ONE HUNDRED TONS OF ICE

ONE HUNDRED TONS OF ICE

AND OTHER GOSPEL STORIES

Lawrence Wood

Westminster John Knox Press
LOUISVILLE • LONDON

All rights reserved. No part of this book may be reproduced or transmitted in any form or by any means, electronic or mechanical, including photocopying, recording, or by any information storage or retrieval system, without permission in writing from the publisher. For information, address Westminster John Knox Press, 100 Witherspoon Street, Louisville, Kentucky 40202-1396.

Scripture quotations, unless otherwise indicated, are from the New Revised Standard Version of the Bible, copyright © 1989 by the Division of Christian Education of the National Council of the Churches of Christ in the U.S.A., and used by permission.

Scripture quotatons marked NEB are taken from *The New English Bible,* © The Delegates of the Oxford University Press and The Syndics of the Cambridge University Press, 1961, 1970. Used by permission.

Scripture quotations marked REB are taken from *The Revised English Bible,* © Oxford University Press and Cambridge University Press, 1989. Used by permission.

Scripture quotations marked RSV are from the Revised Standard Version of the Bible, copyright © 1946, 1952, 1971, and 1973 by the Division of Christian Education of the National Council of the Churches of Christ in the U.S.A., and are used by permission.

See Credits, p. 179, for additional permission information.

Book design by Sharon Adams

First edition
Published by Westminster John Knox Press
Louisville, Kentucky

This book is printed on acid-free paper that meets the American National Standards Institute Z39.48 standard. ♾

PRINTED IN THE UNITED STATES OF AMERICA

03 04 05 06 07 08 09 10 11 12 — 10 9 8 7 6 5 4 3 2 1

Library of Congress Cataloging-in-Publication Data is on file at the Library of Congress, Washington, D.C.

ISBN 0-664-22687-6

This book is for
Rexene and Hannah

Contents

Winter   109

Spring   147

Overture

*M*y friend Dave, to whom things happen, tells this story—in fact, he tells it every chance he gets. "Newfoundlands are a large breed, and ours was very large," he begins. "They're supposed to be friendly and intelligent. Cosmo was . . . a very friendly dog."

Dave and his wife, Shari, were walking the dog on a frozen lake near their place, having heard that a truck had fallen through the ice. The truck, it turned out, was fine, but it didn't take long for Cosmo to venture out too far and fall through, all one hundred and fifty pounds of him. Cursing the dog, cursing himself for letting the dog off the leash, Dave stretched out across the ice on his belly, and just as he came within a foot of rescuing Cosmo he remembered that dogs don't have human shoulders or opposable thumbs to reach for help. Shari stretched out on the ice beside him . . .

Suddenly the ice broke and they were all underwater.

Dave remembers thinking what a stupid way it was to die, as the two of them screamed "for ten seconds or an hour." Somehow he hauled himself out, then Shari. They spent several minutes panting and shivering.

By now all the thin ice had been smashed, and Dave could haul Cosmo out by the scruff of his neck. Cosmo shook as if he had just enjoyed a refreshing swim, and bounded off, frisky as ever.

Covered in frost, Dave and Shari did their best to flag down help. But every time they waved at a car, the people just waved back at the friendly couple and their frisky dog.

Back home in the shower, Dave had two overpowering feelings. The first was that he had just gotten away with something. The second was joy, pure joy. A voice spoke within him: *You belong to God now.*

Thereafter—for weeks, anyway—he felt that all of life was a bonus. A warm towel waited for him after his shower. A bonus! His wife had set the table with sandwiches on paper plates. A bonus! Someone called later in the day about work. A bonus! Monday mornings were a bonus; strangers on the street were a bonus; it was all extra, all given by God. And not the least part of the story is that he told the story, again and again.

—ᴍ—

I believe that's a gospel story. It might not appear in your New Testament, but then again, it could. Good old Mercer Munn, a layman who at ninety years old still drove every night to look for deer, used to tell me, "The last book of the Bible is still being written, and I'd like to add a verse or two."

Maybe that is what preaching is all about—telling the sacred story of our own day. It is wonderful to find that God still talks through us and the people in our lives. A miracle takes place on Sunday mornings as parishioners shuffle into their pews, all very democratic and seemingly very ordinary, and then discover that they are Bible characters. The gospel stories transfigure us.

Up here in the north country evidence of God's work is pretty hard to miss, as are the disparities between rich and poor, the harshness and beauty of the weather, the dramatic changes of seasons. It is a good place to be a preacher. For six years I have gotten up early and driven fifteen miles to worship with prodigal sons, faithful widows, rich fools, people with sick children, and a woman who has been married five times and is living with a sixth man who is not her husband. Ultimately they are all looking for a second chance at life, to know that they are cared for, that they belong to somebody. I have been privileged to enjoy moments of worship with them that cannot be conveyed on the page. If in this book their stories come to life again, then that is a bonus.

Crowded into these pages are friends and strangers and most of all the ancient authors of scripture. God help me if I have taken from any of them lightly.

One man, though, I would like to thank foremost: a beloved teacher, mentor, and friend, Edmund Perry. He was a courtly man with earthy humor, and in closing his phone calls he bade me "Grace and peace." Edmund died in 1998, though our conversations continue. Grace and peace, Edmund.

Summer

Dixon, Illinois

About two hours west of Chicago, west of Wheaton, west of DeKalb, along the Rock River in Lee County, is Dixon, Illinois. The nearest towns are Gap Grove and Prairieville. Highways 88 and 52 intersect near there, as do state roads 26 and 38.

Louella Parsons, the Hollywood gossip columnist, came from Dixon. She attended Dixon High School and Dixon Business College, and served as society editor and drama critic for the Dixon *Sun*. Years later, when she held great power in Hollywood and could make or break careers with a single column, she claimed that she had been high school valedictorian, though there is no record of it. She claimed that she was born in 1893, but that would have meant she graduated at age eight and married at twelve. At the height of her fame, she conveniently forgot marrying her second husband, simply blotted him out of her biography. This woman who ferreted out the most damning secrets of the stars blithely kept her own.

But when she was heard on two hundred and fifty radio stations and was read by forty million readers, she came home for Louella Parsons Day in Dixon.

Ronald Reagan came from Dixon. Just outside his boyhood home, there's a statue of him, a little larger than life. No doubt his childhood there was difficult—with an alcoholic father—but he seems to have been genuinely fond of the place. He always bragged that as a lifeguard there he saved seventy-seven people, spoke wistfully of the folks who called him "Dutch," and wrote in his autobiography that "one of the benefits of my success in Holly-wood was being invited to visit Dixon for the annual Petunia Festival."

Why did stars like Louella Parsons and Ronald Reagan return so readily? There is no evidence that they had kept up with friends.

Maybe they just needed to see how far they had come, how high they had risen, and were reassured before they went back home to Beverly Hills or the hills above Malibu.

—⁊⁊⁊—

One of the first persons who heard reports about Jesus of Nazareth asked, "Can anything good come out of Nazareth?" Compared to the big neighboring city of Sepphoris, Nazareth was nothing. It was a small town set upon a hill; despite its obscurity, however, Jesus observed that "a city on a hill cannot be hid." Mountains could be seen in three directions, a low plain to the south. Modest rainfall allowed for growing fruits, grains, and vegetables, but the town had only one spring, perhaps the "Well of Mary" that is shown to tourists. Altogether, a very ordinary place.

And yet Jesus came from Nazareth, by accident or providence.

Our scriptures tell us a little about his roots. It seems that while significant events (his birth, his baptism, his temptation) took place elsewhere, he always came home:

> They returned to Galilee, to their own town of Nazareth. The child grew and became strong, filled with wisdom; and the favor of God was upon him. (*Luke 2:39–40*)

> Then Jesus, filled with the power of the Spirit, returned to Galilee, and a report about him spread through all the surrounding country. He began to teach in the synagogues and was praised by everyone. (*Luke 4:14–15*)

It's curious that the scriptures don't say, "Filled with the Holy Spirit, he went to Jerusalem." Wouldn't that have been the usual and expected thing for a promising young man to do? Returning to Nazareth wasn't the route to success. Even his own brothers wouldn't accept him until he had made his name elsewhere: "Leave here and go to Judea so that your disciples also may see the works you are doing; for no one who wants to be widely known acts in secret. If you do these things, show yourself to the world" (John 7:3–4).

One of the most amazing gospel stories tells how he was literally chased out of town by people who had known him all his life. Curious about his reputation as a charismatic healer, they all had turned out to hear him at the synagogue, and he read from the prophet Isaiah:

> "The Spirit of the Lord is upon me, because he has anointed me to bring good news to the poor. He has sent me to proclaim release to the captives, and recovery of sight to the blind, to let the oppressed go free, to proclaim the year of the Lord's favor." (Luke 4:18–19)

Then he said, "Today this scripture has been fulfilled in your hearing." To his neighbors, this was not only blasphemous, it was personally insulting. He thought they were poor? captive? blind? Nor were they impressed when he reminded them about the abuse that the prophets had received from their hometowns. Well, if he wanted to set himself up as a prophet, they would oblige. They rose and drove him to the brow of the hill on which their town was built, and tried to throw him off.

Now you or I, after such a narrow escape, would no longer want to think of that place as home. But because Jesus loved differently than you or I, he took its name with him. When the crowds cheered him on Palm Sunday, they called him "Jesus *of Nazareth.*" When he was crucified, the sign above him read "Jesus *of Nazareth.*"

—⚍—

With all respect to stage and screen, there really is a difference between a "superstar" and Jesus. A star seems to signify the distance between fame and anonymity; he or she has "made it," has "gotten out" or "escaped." Jesus never made it, or got out, or escaped, but remained among his people, and drew his disciples from his region. (The only disciple not from Galilee was Judas Iscariot.)

A star courts and flatters the hometown folks, and for whatever reasons still seeks their approval. Jesus did no such thing. Flattery can mask contempt, whereas Jesus' candor came from love.

A star seems so much finer than us, seems to surpass us—but really is just like us, as inevitably we find out. Louella Parsons and Ronald Reagan made mistakes, conveniently forgot some of the details. Everybody is human. Jesus, however, was something more. He surpassed and transcended human life to show us the realm of God. And if he really was our Lord and God, then his companions were all the more wonderful.

Simon, Andrew, James, and John weren't from the big city, either. They were fishermen from nearby, and it's likely that they had known Jesus for years before he said, "Follow me." Matthew hailed from Capernaum, Philip from Bethsaida, Bartholomew from Cana. Occasionally these men disappointed him, but he stuck by them and entrusted them with the secret of who he was.

He rose from the dead, sought these same humble men, and sent them back to their region of Galilee. He himself returned to Galilee and met them on a mountaintop. From there they could see everything—the plains, the fruit trees, the fields, the rivers, the inland sea, the larger cities, and the city on a hill.

—∿∿—

Ed Eichenberger came from Dixon. It's likely you've never heard of him; he's a retired dentist who now lives in my small town in northern Michigan. A few years ago he went back there, to discover some of his own past, and found it small and ill-kept and depressed. There still were remnants of the shoe factory, the wire screen factory, the cement plant.

And yet, while much of the landscape was unlovely, it was possible to see some of what Chief Black Hawk had cherished in the Rock River valley—the river banks overgrown with oak, black walnut, willow, wild plum, thornapple trees, berries, and grapes, the small hills above the Midwestern plains.

Sometimes we love a place because it needs so much to be loved.

Jesus was not from Chicago. He ended his ministry in the big city—he was killed there—but his ministry really was in Nazareth and Capernaum and Bethany, in DeKalb and Moline and Rockford and Dixon. He was of those places, and over and above them, not in the way of a star or celebrity, but of God.

The world will never get over the shock that the one true God was also a man in Dixon, Illinois—in a city that could not be hid.

Where It Comes from, Where It Goes

*T*he Jordan River is the lowest river in the world. Its headwaters come from Mt. Hermon, the highest mountain in Palestine, which rises almost two thousand feet taller than any other in the region, and fully nine thousand feet above sea level. The very name Hermon means "sacred," and according to the gospels, this was the sacred mountain where Jesus was transfigured.

Melted snow runs from these slopes down to the valley in swift tributaries. Once upon a time they passed through a papyrus marsh and a shallow lake. Then the waters of the Jordan dropped even more sharply through a narrow gorge, seven hundred feet below sea level to the inland Sea of Galilee. Here farmers tilled the fertile banks and fishermen packed their catch into salt barrels, in towns such as Capernaum, which lay nearest the mouth of the river; scandalous Magdala; and Tiberias, a Gentile city founded in Jesus' lifetime by the Romans.

People washed their clothes in the water, bathed in it, relieved themselves in it.

South of Galilee, the Jordan River wandered for two hundred miles toward its end only sixty-five miles away. For most of the route the river valley was flanked on either side by steep mountain walls. Even over this short distance the climate changed dramatically, the mountains gave way to badlands, and soon the Jordan flowed through a desert, ending, significantly enough, in the Dead Sea.

Six miles north of the Dead Sea, according to tradition, Jesus came to these waters and was baptized.

High and low, pure and foul, sacred waters from a sacred source mingled with the effluent of human life—could any waters be more appropriate for Jesus' baptism?

—〜〜—

Where do we come from, and where are we going? Pilgrims traveled far into the desert seeking answers to these questions. They willingly went back into a desert wilderness such as their ancestors had left to meet the God of their ancestors; they set aside all claims of heritage to establish for themselves a right relationship with God; they submitted to the same baptism required of Gentile converts to Judaism, and were washed by John in the river Jordan.

Most likely they had some trouble in getting there. They had to pack and load animals for the journey and be on the lookout for wolves and thieves. It was not a trip for the merely curious. For Jews especially to make this trip required some moral courage. But once they arrived, this is what they got from John: "You brood of vipers! Who warned you to flee from the wrath to come? Bear fruit worthy of repentance." According to John, they had come from sin and were going to hell.

Then out of that crowd stepped someone John recognized—his cousin Jesus—and instantly his tone changed. "I need to be baptized by you, not you by me," John protested. Jesus asked to be baptized anyway. He stepped into the river amid sinners who had been told they did not deserve to be called Jews, and joined them in an act of repentance. That is what baptism meant. He repented.

At this, so the gospels say, the heavens opened—that is, it rained in that desert. Rain soaked into the parched ground and a voice said, "This is my child, my beloved, with whom I am well pleased."

—〜〜—

There are those who say that Jesus was sinless, that he had nothing for which to repent. I wonder, though. Nowhere in the gospels does he make such claims for himself. In fact, he tells one admirer, "Why do you call me good? Only God is good." He asks a person who brings him a dispute, "Who set me up as a judge or arbiter over you?" At times his anger and frustration seem very much like our own. Clearly he is innocent of a crime, falsely condemned. But my faith has never needed him to be a spotless lamb. Rather, I have needed Jesus to be one of us.

How else could he stand us? Our food, our smells, our jokes, our worries? Each day his feet were caked with dust. His bowels moved. It all must have been a rank offense to him *unless he was one of us*. In which case it wouldn't have been enough to wash in our waters; no, like us, he would have wanted to be bathed in the Spirit and be reborn.

If John saw us first as sinners, Jesus saw us as children of God, and maybe that's why he was comfortable with us, impure and imperfect though we are. Perhaps he saw in us a fundamental goodness beyond perfection.

It's possible that he himself was perfect, but then again maybe not. After all, baptism meant repentance, and it's hard to believe that he simply went through the motions; that would have been almost blasphemous. In any event, for us, his disciples, the Christian life is not about sinlessness, but faithfulness—about a personal relationship with God. (John was right about this: it's not enough for us to hide behind our grandparents' faith. We need our own. Even Jesus did.)

Jesus of Nazareth, the son of Mary and Joseph, the student of the Torah and religious pilgrim, came from God and was going where the Spirit led him. His ministry began with this baptism; it took him past other people's mistakes and misfortunes, past judgment or regret. It took him deeper and deeper into the world of sin and sinners, until at last it took his life. On the riverbank he stepped with the crowd, then from the crowd; he identified with us, then submitted to a Spirit beyond us.

"The wind blows where it wills, and you hear the sound of it, but you do not know whence it comes or whither it goes; so it is with every one who is born of the Spirit." (John 3:8 RSV)

Jesus bathed in the river Jordan as a sign of repentance, but much more significantly he bathed in the Spirit and began a new life.

—w—

The tap water in my town comes from four wells, two of them artesian. The water is a very cold forty-two degrees, and testing confirms that it comes not from Lake Michigan, which is just a hundred yards away, but Lake Superior, over a hundred miles away. Harbor Springs is known for its springs—hence the name—and indeed there are artesian wells all over town in yards and basements. Entrepreneurs have even thought to bottle our water because it's so pure.

We use this water to cook, bathe, wash paintbrushes, and carry away our sewage. Our wastewater gets pumped out of town and, believe it or not, is sprayed onto cornfields by giant snowmaking machines retired from the nearby ski hills. This removes some dangerous nitrates; natural filtration in the ground is supposed to do the rest. Eventually this water will work its way back into the Great Lakes to become tap water in another town.

I pour tap water into a porcelain bowl in making ready for a home baptism. Just in case it's too pure, I add a little holy water from the Jordan. A wife and her bedridden husband have asked me into this upstairs bedroom where he is dying of brain cancer. Flushed and shirtless, he no longer troubles to hide his lesions. A few years ago he was self-sufficient, well-to-do, but until finding this faith, he never felt worthy of love—not in his first marriage, and not always in his second. He has plenty of sins to confess.

Now he's ready to embrace his new life. He hasn't come to this accidentally; it has been his decision. (John was right about this: nobody can take your bath for you.)

He props himself up on a pillow and laughs a little at himself for the emotion of the moment. We three share a prayer and a scripture reading, and his wife edges closer.

"Are you ready for this?" I ask.

"Yes. Yes," he says strongly.

I wet my hand in the basin, press it lightly on his forehead, speak his name, and say, "I baptize you in the name of the Father, the Son, and the Holy Spirit."

Tears wet his face, and over again he repeats, "I'm a child of God." Today the heavens have opened and rains fall on his parched heart.

It's never too late for us to find that we come from God, that we are his children. We are passing through all that is human—work, waste, washing—and are going back to him, to the Father of waters, the source of life. It's never too late to hear words that John might not have heard, but Jesus did:

"This is my child, my beloved, with whom I am well pleased."

Fall of Man

*E*veryone has a story. I hated church as a boy; it bored me beyond belief. It wasn't because I had trouble sitting still—well, sure, we kids might rattle pencils in the pew rack, fight and giggle, or lean too close to the backs of people's heads, or lie down. Really I hated to go because I could think holes in the Sunday school stories. A flood that covered mountains? A man inside a fish? Why grown people went in for this was beyond me. As soon as I was old enough I insisted on staying home.

After all, my father often stayed home. An agnostic, he liked to drink his coffee and read the Sunday paper in the quiet of an empty household. Once I turned sixteen, with my life becoming my own in every other respect, I joined him and firmly refused to attend church. I had so many philosophical objections that it actually seemed wrong to go. Even when my father went with the rest of the family, I stayed home on principle.

One Sunday in May I woke up especially late. Everyone else had dressed and eaten a big breakfast of my father's waffles. I stayed out of their way and sat in my pajamas at the kitchen table pretending to be absorbed in the newspaper. They all got into the car and it thrummed in the driveway for a good ten minutes. Then Dad came back inside.

"We're leaving for church now," he said.

"Have a good time," I said, and returned to the newspaper.

Dad said, "We're all going today. All the family. It's Mother's Day."

I sighed and put down the paper long enough to explain that I was tired from the night before, and that I didn't like church and was old enough to make my own decisions.

"Your mother really wants you to go."

And at that, I evilly said, "Look, I don't care if they're taking a count, I'm not going to win some contest for her today."

He went back outside. They all waited a long while before pulling away.

Well, I don't know that I have ever made a bigger waste of time. I didn't even enjoy myself. The paper no longer was as interesting; the waffles didn't taste as good. Surely my feelings of guilt were their fault. Why shouldn't I be permitted to enjoy a Sunday morning as I pleased? The hour passed a little too quickly, too. Before I'd done anything pleasant, purposeful or even very relaxing, the car crunched in the driveway again, and I hurried upstairs. I heard the back door open and my family come in. Then footsteps on the stairs—not my brother's or my sisters', but my father's. He didn't come to my room. He turned the other way and went into a bathroom and closed the door. What I heard next was a strange and terrible sound. He sobbed. I had never heard him cry before.

—w—

Everybody has a story. There once was a man in the town of Jericho hated by his neighbors, for he collaborated with the occupying Romans, collected taxes, and cheated his own people. A little man in every regard, he lined his pockets and earned only scorn. There's no particular reason that two thousand years later we should know his name, but we do. He was Zacchaeus.

A holy man with a growing reputation, said by some to be the Messiah, was to pass through Jericho. If he really was the Messiah, then it would be lights out for the Romans, the end to their hated occupation of Palestine and the beginning of new greatness for the Jews. Crowds lined the streets to see him, touch him, taunt him, or simply wonder. We take him for granted, but it is remarkable that all these years later we know his name: Jesus.

Among the curious was Zacchaeus. The thick crowds and his small stature made it difficult for him to glimpse this purported Messiah. Still he knew how to find an advantage, and climbed a sycamore tree.

> Jesus entered Jericho and was passing through it. A man was there named Zacchaeus; he was a chief tax collector and was rich. He was trying to see who Jesus was, but on account of the crowd he could not, because he was short in stature. So he ran ahead and climbed a sycamore tree to see him, because he was going to pass that way. When Jesus came to the place, he looked up and said to him, "Zacchaeus, hurry and come down; for I must stay at your house today." (Luke 19:1–5)

Jesus knew his name! How did he know his name? The crowd murmured its disapproval, and surely no one was more surprised or puzzled than Zacchaeus. *You came for me? Why me?* Why would a Jewish Messiah come for him?

But Jesus had. Zacchaeus hurried down to welcome him—a changed man by the time his feet reached the ground, in a hurry not only to welcome this wonderful guest but to put right many wrongs he had done. Before Zacchaeus worried about preparing dinner or turning down a bed, he talked about changing his life, right there in front of everybody. He was in a state of grace.

Some of us are brought down by gravity, and some come down by grace. I think we all would prefer the latter, but so few of us ever realize our loftiness, our precariousness, until we come down with a good hard thump. It's not the fall, but what happens next that makes all the difference.

Jesus declared, "Salvation has come to this house today." An astounding claim, considering that a Messiah was supposed to save an entire country all at once, with armies and trumpets that would level mighty fortresses. No, Jesus was going to do it one person at a time. This little man Zacchaeus, a nobody, a Roman collaborator, was saved by a relationship with him. That day in Jericho, the walls came tumbling down.

—⁊⁊⁊—

My junior year of college, some friends invited me to join them on our dormitory roof to take pictures of the Chicago skyline. Actually, only one of us would be taking pictures—my good friend Carl, already a real photojournalist. So we lugged his tripod and gear to the fifth-floor deck called "the beach," then up a series of steeply pitched roofs, our sneakers sliding on the shingles. Once up there, what a beautiful evening we saw! A great night to be alive! For hours we marveled as Lake Michigan, the campus, and the city blazed in the setting sun.

Once it got dark, Carl needed help getting down, so I shimmied down to the deck, where I could see the others and offer directions. To get a better view, I backed up . . . and backed up . . . nearer to an opening in the wall to a fire escape . . . and then walked right off the roof.

As I plummeted, several thoughts went through my head—each very clear and definite.

I thought, "This is it. This is how my life ends."

I thought, "I am not going to finish anything I was doing today."

It was almost ironic.

I felt calm.

Then suddenly my fall was broken by the fire escape. How I held onto it, God knows—I can't remember—but the next thing I knew, that was where I lay. The fall had broken all my ribs and punctured a lung. It was almost impossible to call for help. With great difficulty I managed one small howl. It took a long time to attract help, and finally paramedics came, lifted and lowered me by a stretcher to the ambulance, cut the clothes off me, and took me to the hospital, where I lay for hours on a gurney.

When I woke up, I was amazed to find myself there and to remember what had happened. I tried to recall what day it was. It was Sunday.

It was Easter Sunday, 1986.

—ᵐ—

Some of us are brought down by gravity, and some come down by grace. I can testify to both ways. What happens after a fall is often as dramatic as the fall itself.

The real drama of that day in Jericho was not that the local tax collector got found out in a sycamore tree, but that every relationship in his life was different when he came down. Townspeople could hardly believe what they saw or heard. There was still a man among them who went by the name Zacchaeus, but he was a changed man:

> All who saw it began to grumble and said, "He has gone to be the guest of one who is a sinner." Zacchaeus stood there and said to the Lord, "Look, half of my possessions, Lord, I will give to the poor; and if I have defrauded anyone of anything, I will pay back four times as much." Then Jesus said to him, "Today salvation has come to this house, because he too is a son of Abraham. For the Son of Man came to seek out and to save the lost." (Luke 19:7–10)

Salvation came to that house *that* day. Not on Good Friday, not on Easter Sunday—but that day in Jericho, as Zacchaeus was saved and changed by a relationship with Christ.

The trees are full of people who have not yet found that relationship. Some, of course, haven't been to church; others have been going to church all their lives and they're still up in the trees. Maybe you're sitting up there right now, carefully observing, waiting to decide. You thought you could keep your distance, get a peek without being seen, but listen, listen to him—he wants you to come on down!

Who, me?

Yes, you.

He knows my name?

Yes. He knows your name.

Swing Time

We remember Fred Astaire best from his movies with Ginger Rogers—*Swing Time, Top Hat, Flying Down to Rio.* If you have never seen his later films, you will be simply amazed by the witty imagination of his dances with coat racks, picture frames, sofas, all kinds of unlikely partners. S'wonderful, s'marvelous, how he moved so effortlessly, so gracefully.

We remember him as a dancer, yet he was also a lover of horses, and for many years he kept a stable of thoroughbreds. Late in his life, he fell in love with a female jockey named Robyn Smith. She had been on the cover of *Sports Illustrated,* hailed as "a sensation in silks." She also loved him, and in 1980, when he was eighty-one and she was thirty-five, they married.

After seven happy years, Fred died. Robyn remembers his death in veterinary terms: "He never complained, but I noticed he was breathing faster, and his nostrils were flared. He was terribly dehydrated because he had gone off his feed."

Fred's will, by the way, made her executor of his estate and left his film clips entirely in her hands. While others owned movies shown in their entirety, Fred had retained the rights to his clips, and he had told Robyn, "I've been taken advantage of all my life. Please don't let them take advantage of me. And I know you won't. I'm leaving you in charge because I trust you implicitly."

In December of 1992, the Kennedy Center in Washington prepared to honor Ginger Rogers for her career in film—just as they had honored Fred before. Ginger was an old and dear friend, but Robyn refused to release any film clips for broadcast. TV audiences, who had to watch Ginger in her dramatic roles, wondered where Fred was.

A few years later, they found out where Fred was. He was dancing not with Ginger, but with a Dirt Devil vacuum cleaner. Thanks to digital processing, the coat rack and picture frame from *Royal Wedding* and *Easter Parade* had been erased and replaced with a Broom Vac and Hand Vac, so that he appeared to be cleaning with debonair *joie de vie*.

After the ads made their debut, Royal Corporation, the makers of Dirt Devil, received a letter from Ava McKenzie, Fred Astaire's daughter: "Your paltry, unconscionable commercials are the antithesis of everything my lovely, gentle father represented. I am saddened that after his wonderful career, he was sold to the devil."

Ms. McKenzie also returned her own Dirt Devil with the letter. She wrote, "Our housekeeper discovered that it has just stopped working. I feel that my father was telling me something."

—␣␣—

Something similar has happened to Jesus. Here was a radical man, a prophet of such power that the authorities had to crucify him. Yet over the centuries he has grown more familiar and less threatening, so ever-present, so commercial that even persons with entirely the wrong ideas about his message claim him as their own.

He is used to sell an institutional church far removed from his way of life, to sell books, videos, even holy trinkets at special times of the year. Perhaps you have seen Ricardo Montalban on TV selling crucifix jewelry, only $39.95 for "a priceless Trinity Cross." I can't imagine Jesus selling this cross or any other. It's not just tacky, it's graceless. It's the power of the Dirt Devil.

Of course, Jesus was misunderstood in his own day, a point stressed by all four gospels, particularly the gospel of John: "He was in the world, and the world was made through him, yet the world knew him not" (John 1:10 RSV).

People asked, "Is this not Jesus, the son of Joseph, whose father and mother we know? How does he now say, 'I have come down from heaven'?" "How is it that this man has learning, when he has never studied?" They asked, "Who are you?"

When he was about to leave his disciples, and his identity problem was about to become their own, Jesus said,

"And I will pray the Father, and he will give you another Counselor, to be with you for ever, even the Spirit of truth, whom the world cannot receive, because it neither sees him nor knows him; you know him, for he dwells with you, and will be in you." (John 14:16–17 RSV)

In other words, he gave them the same assurances he had been given, that in an uncomprehending world they would not be lonely. Someone would remind them who they were.

Now that the church is often mistaken for a business, and the cross may be seen as just another corporate logo, it's essential that we know who we are. This is an important time for us; it is a Swing Time. The church could go this way or that, either toward what is meaningless or what is meaningful; toward what is deadly or what is lively. It's essential that we know a real, three-dimensional, flesh-and-blood Christ, because we're saved by knowing him.

What do young people today know of Fred Astaire? His face and name, maybe. A few may recognize the name Ginger Rogers. Only one or two here and there have watched his classic routines in *Swing Time*, *Top Hat*, *Shall We Dance?*, *Holiday Inn*, *Flying Down to Rio*, *The Band Wagon*, and *Easter Parade*. The vividness of the man, the fullness of his talent, has been reduced to an icon or a symbol.

Which brings me to an old show-business joke, the four ages of Fred:

First they say, "Get me Fred Astaire!"

Then they say, "Get me a young Fred Astaire!"

Then it's, "Get me a Fred Astaire type!"

And lastly, "Who's Fred Astaire?"

That's what happens to fame. The greater and more original you are, the more the world tries to reduce you.

What do young people know today of Jesus? They know his name. Maybe they have learned a few memorable Bible episodes. A generous handful might know of Peter and Paul. Do they really know Jesus in any real and human sense? Do we? Or is he, for us as well, merely an image, an icon, a symbol?

If that is true, then it is the work of a devil—the Dirt Devil. The Dirt Devil takes what is human and holy and full of meaning and reduces it to a shadow of its former self, so that someone else might profit instead of God.

Now, the power of a Dirt Devil is considerable. It fits in the palm of your hand and in your back pocket. It sucks up money when bookstores sell Christian knick-knacks, when televangelists sell videotapes about the end times, when religious political action committees sell power. None of this has anything to do with the man from Nazareth or the way he lived his life.

In the scriptures we meet a man who owned nothing, not even his own soul, for that too belonged to God. "Foxes have holes, birds of the air have nests, but the Son of Man has nowhere to lay his head," he said. He devoted his life to preparing for the kingdom of God, even though he did not know when it would come. Few people considered him the Messiah, and although he performed wondrous miracles of healing and even raised the dead, he refused to save himself.

It's all there in the Bible, and he is still saving people, yet this Jesus is not famous. He remains in obscurity, even though his name is heard everywhere.

—∿∿—

About the same time that Fred Astaire was dancing with Ginger, James Agee was writing about the Depression poor, in a book called *Let Us Now Praise Famous Men*. He wrote:

Every fury on earth has been absorbed in time, as art, or religion, or as authority in one form or another. The deadliest blow the enemy of the human soul can strike is to do fury honor. Swift, Blake, Beethoven, Christ . . . name me a one who has not been thus castrated. Official acceptance is the unmistakable sign that salvation is beaten again, and is the one surest sign of fatal misunderstanding, and is the kiss of Judas.[1]

The title of Agee's book came from Ecclesiasticus (or Sirach), a book of the Apocrypha written by Jesus, the son of Sirach, who lived almost two centuries before Jesus of Nazareth. It was translated from the Hebrew into Greek by his grandson, who chose to remain anonymous. Like all scripture, it is both ancient and timeless as it honors the men and women, famous and obscure, who gave us an inheritance of faith:

Let us now praise famous men, and our fathers in their generations . . . leaders of the people in their deliberations and in understanding of learning for the people, wise in their words of instruction; those who composed musical tunes, and set forth verses in writing; rich men furnished with resources, living peaceably in their habitations—all these were honored in their generations, and were the glory of their times. There are some of them who have left a name, so that men declare their praise.

And there were some who have no memorial, who have perished as though they had not been born, and so have their children after them. But these were men of mercy, whose righteous deeds have not been forgotten; their prosperity will remain with their descendants, and their inheritance to their children's children. Their descendants stand by the covenants; their children also, for their sake. Their posterity will continue for ever, and their glory will not be blotted out. Their bodies were buried in peace, and their name lives to all generations. People will declare their wisdom, and the congregations proclaim their praise. (Ecclesiasticus 44:1–15)

Fame or obscurity, they were all the same to Jesus of Nazareth. He was mindful not of image, but reality, and gave himself over to the high art of holiness, regardless of what others made of him.

If they misunderstood, he was not surprised. No one had ever shown such grace before. Now we become his partners—a role for which we could never be truly prepared. We dance with the Lord of the Dance, and take hold of his hands as we learn the basic steps.

Cinnamon and Sugar

Some tastes stay with you. Rexene and I can vividly recall our first date, when she drank, and pretended to enjoy, her first cup of coffee. This time of the year, we can feel those first stirrings of love all over again.

However, honesty compels me to admit that the sincerest love is for food. When we humans love each other, we have mixed motives, but my love for pound cake is pretty uncomplicated. As evidence, I'm beginning to get love handles. Apparently my father decided not to keep his pair.

Gingerbread, coffeecake, shortbread and scones, I love them indiscriminately—and also one of Rexene's favorites, cinnamon rolls. The recipe, as given in the *Better Homes and Gardens* cookbook, is faintly erotic—all the ingredients are in italics, *for emphasis*, I guess.

Melt 3 tablespoons *butter*; brush half the butter over the dough. Combine one-half cup *sugar* and 2 teaspoons ground *cinnamon*; sprinkle half of mixture over dough. Roll up from one of the long sides. Seal seams. Slice dough into 12 pieces. Place rolls in two greased nine-inch round baking pans, cover and let rise till nearly double (about 30 minutes). Bake in a 375° oven for 20 to 25 minutes. Cool slightly. Drizzle with *powdered sugar icing* . . .

My God! It's impossible to read this aloud without sounding lascivious.

Well, now. You may have heard somewhere that there are only four basic tastes: sweet, sour, bitter, salty. This isn't exactly true; actually, scientists now aren't sure how many basic tastes there are. We can tell a difference among sweeteners, for example. We can tell cane sugar from corn syrup, maple syrup, or honey.

In any event, the taste of cinnamon is complex—warm, slightly bitter, slightly sweet. The taste of sugar is simple and basic—it's just sweet. Together, cinnamon and sugar complement each other. The cinnamon gives depth to the sugar, and you couldn't eat the cinnamon without the sugar.

If you're married, chances are that your marriage tastes like cinnamon and sugar. Maybe you yourself supply one flavor or the other, or maybe you trade them back and forth.

These flavors come from different ends of the earth—cinnamon from Sri Lanka, sugar from the Caribbean and Hawaii. Goodness knows how they first got together. They represent two kinds of loving.

—⚯—

The First Letter of John is not as erotic as, say, the Song of Songs, but it gives us quite a taste of love—something mighty strong. Of course you might not be prepared for it if you're just used to flowers, kisses, and bare skin. Real love gets its strong flavor from God: "We love because God first loved us."

Much of what we call love is conditional. We have to earn it; it has strings attached; it makes us anxious. But that is not at all what love should be like. As John says, "There is no fear in love, but perfect love casts out fear." So God takes the initiative in his strong-willed way, and loves us even when we are not trying to be lovable. John goes so far as to say that God *is* love, which should tell us right there that the real thing is not a mushy, sentimental, greeting-card feeling, but an expression of will.

God *chooses* to love us. That's what makes all other real love possible.

"You did not choose me, but I chose you," Jesus said. He made no conditions on what he chose to do; he simply did it, perhaps because in any given moment, most relationships are unequal, and because he was willing to do it until we chose to respond.

There is a difference between "being in love" and loving. "Being in love" is passive. It's like sugar—it's sweet, everybody likes it, too much of it probably isn't good for us. But willing oneself to love another is like cinnamon—it makes for complexity and depth, even though by itself it's a little bitter and unpleasant.

In his book *Love and Will*, psychologist Rollo May said that "in the long run, love and will are present together in each genuine act." Along those same lines, Scott Peck has written that

> the person who truly loves does so because of a decision to love. This person has made a commitment to be loving whether or not the loving feeling is present. If it is, so much the better; but if it isn't, the commitment to love, the will to love, still stands. . . . True love is not a feeling by which we are overwhelmed. It is a committed, thoughtful decision.[2]

These two feelings—loving and being in love—need each other. Being in love without the will to love is child's play. And having the will to love without being in love is just hard work. Few of us could remain in such relationships forever.

One without the other is a prelude to adultery.

In the Book of Proverbs, we find another mention of cinnamon—and here it is a spice of seduction. The poor young man, who knows only about being in love and nothing about having the will to love, is dragged against his will straight into an affair:

> From the window of my house I have seen a young man without sense, passing along the street near her corner, taking the road to her house in the twilight, in the evening, at the time of night and darkness. And lo, a woman meets him. She is loud and wayward, her feet do not stay at home; now in the street, now in the market, and at every corner she lies in wait. She seizes him and kisses him and says:
>
> "I have decked my couch with coverings, colored spreads of Egyptian linen; I have perfumed my bed with myrrh, aloes, and cinnamon. Come, let us take our fill of love till morning, let us delight ourselves with love. For my husband is not at home; he has gone on a long journey. . . ." With much seductive speech she persuades him; with her smooth talk she compels him. All at once he follows her, as an ox goes to the slaughter . . . he does not know that it will cost him his life. Prov. 7:6–27 RSV, adapted)

To be sure, not every slip in our married life ends that badly, but we do know that when we have forgotten the will to love, great, great pain has happened, and we have been dragged against our will where we did not want to go.

Together, loving and being in love provide strength, and tell us that God is good—good enough to delight our senses and fill our hearts. But don't take just my word. If you want corroboration, ask that sweet gray-haired couple; ask this athletic young couple; ask any two people who have really worked at a marriage and can say with the psalmist, "Taste and see that the Lord is good."

—⌇⌇—

Now that Rexene and I share our marriage with a toddler, we don't get a lot of sleep, or anything else, for that matter. She gets up with Hannah early, and then crawls back under the covers, and soon we both fall out of bed for good.

Yesterday we got up more or less together and tottered downstairs to breakfast. We were not especially beautiful. She had, let us say, hydrangea hair and no makeup. I wore pajama bottoms that showed my love handles. (They're called love handles because you have to *will* yourself to love them—you wouldn't call them lust handles.)

We smelled a little stale as we went downstairs and fixed cinnamon rolls. Not from scratch, mind you; from a can.

So there we were, not talking, both a little too tired and grumpy to talk. From the oven we could smell the rising yeast, and the cinnamon, and the sugar.

Those rolls were so good—warm, still kind of moist, the icing runny. You know, we felt good. We didn't *look* good, but we felt good. And we chose each other all over again.

That's what a marriage is, really—choosing each other again, on a daily basis. Some days you feel like it, and some days you don't. That is the recipe, and I can't promise you that any other way will turn out. Let me just say that we got this old recipe from a good source, and we try to have it often at our house.

A Sticky Situation

A friend of mine got into a little mess. He was engaged to be married; the relationship was, shall we say, unequal. For eight long years, she had patiently waited for marriage; for eight long years, he had eluded it, sometimes suggesting that she would be happier with someone else. They had broken up more than once. At last he underwent a change of heart—he grew up, I guess—and proposed. He bought a ring, threw himself into the wedding plans, and came quite readily to premarital counseling.

That was where she announced to me that he had slept with her best friend. She had found out from the friend. He hung his head in shame, immobilized, wishing to be somewhere, anywhere else, but was stuck there on that sofa in my office.

"That was a long time ago," he said.

"*I just found out yesterday*," she said.

It takes a long time to clean up after a mess like that.

—⁘—

Over eighty years ago, Boston had a warm winter spell. It was only two degrees above zero on January 12, 1919, but on the thirteenth, the temperature shot up forty degrees and stayed there. By mid-week, folks were out in their shirtsleeves, taking picnic lunches to the waterfront of Boston's North End, and on Commercial Street,

a few intrepid souls climbed up the sides of a big, warm molasses
tank owned by the Purity Distilling Company.

Just one more state was needed to ratify the Eighteenth Amendment; in a hurry to make rum before Prohibition, the company had
filled the vat to its maximum, two-and-a-half-million gallons of
molasses.

Firemen across the street at the No. 3 Pump House were taking
lunch and shooting billiards; a little girl named Maria DiStasio was
gathering firewood; motorcars and horse-drawn wagons were
going to and fro. No one knew that the warm winter weather had
strained the rivets and weakened the seams of the molasses tank—
until the rivets popped, like machine-gun fire. The next day's
newspaper would describe "a dull, muffled roar that gave but an
instant's warning before the top of the tank was blown into the air."

A thirty-foot wave of hot molasses instantly solidified those in
its path. The little girl carrying firewood was turned into a statue.
A wagon driver cooked to death, still holding his reins. Horses
were carried in its wake, and a boy was almost carried out to sea
until a quick-thinking man reached out with a pole and pulled him
to safety. The molasses even knocked down trestles for the ele-
vated train.

The *New York Times* would note:

> The greatest mortality apparently occurred in one of the city
> buildings, where a score of municipal workers were eating their
> lunch. The building was demolished and the wreckage was
> hurled fifty yards. The other city building, which had an office
> on the ground floor and a tenement above, was similarly torn
> from its foundations.
>
> One of the sections of the tank wall fell on the firehouse
> known as the Engine, which was nearby. The building was
> crushed and three firemen were buried in the ruins . . . [3]

The Great Molasses Flood, one of the most bizarre disasters
ever, killed twenty-one and injured one hundred and fifty. Survivors had to have their clothes cut off them; horses had to be shot.
Even in its aftermath, the flood presented a sticky situation, for the
molasses stood three feet deep. Policemen in blue, Army soldiers

in green, and Red Cross volunteers in white, all were soon to be brown and indistinguishable. They tried to remove the molasses with hoes and brooms, tried to wash it away with freshwater from fire hydrants, all to no avail. Progress came only when fireboats pumped saltwater from the Harbor.

And even more strange, on the second day relief efforts all stopped as church bells rang downtown: Nebraska had ratified the Eighteenth Amendment.

Months later, the people of Boston were still finding that molasses had been tracked all over the city and outlying areas from Gloucester to Concord. It was on doorknobs, trolley seats, benches, and sidewalks, and telephones stuck to their hands and ears. Through the summer, Boston Harbor remained a deep shade of brown—and the odor! There are those who swear that on a hot summer day in the North End, you can still smell it.

—⁓—

We get ourselves into the worst and most bizarre predicaments. And we rarely foresee them; we can't imagine that the weather might change quickly and split everything wide open. I think of my friend who had ended his affair—probably even thought that he had kept it contained—and then out came all the rivets and a deadly mess.

The old word for this is sin. When we are stuck in it, we fear that we will never be free or clean again.

Fortunately, that is not the last word. God is gracious, and our worst moments are occasions for his best. God cleanses, repairs, and rebuilds our families and friendships, for God knows that they need us, and we need them.

The last word in our lives is not sin, but grace.

Grace is the love that takes us by surprise. It's the help we hadn't counted on, the kindness we didn't think we deserved. And maybe we don't, but it's there anyway, and this is how we survive most of our disasters. I'm thinking of David, the great, beloved king, who forgot himself and used his power to take Bathsheba, another man's wife. Of course, grace wasn't what he received at first; he had to face the consequences of what he'd done. He had gotten her pregnant. He had, let's face it, killed her cuckolded husband. And when the consequences came, they were just as wild and cruel as his own behavior—for not he, but his infant son died.

King David was indeed a pathetic figure, abased in grief, not eating or sleeping for the seven days that his boy lay dying.

> The servants of David were afraid to tell him that the child was dead; for they said, "While the child was still alive, we spoke to him, and he did not listen to us; how then can we tell him the child is dead? He may do himself some harm." But when David saw that his servants were whispering together, he perceived that the child was dead; and David said to his servants, "Is the child dead?" They said, "He is dead."
>
> Then David rose from the ground, washed, anointed himself, and changed his clothes. He went into the house of the LORD, and worshiped; he then went to his own house; and when he asked, they set food before him and he ate. Then his servants said to him, "What is this thing you have done? You fasted and wept for the child while it was alive; but when the child died, you rose and ate food." He said, "While the child was still alive, I fasted and wept; for I said, 'Who knows? The LORD may be gracious to me, and the child may live.' But now he is dead; why should I fast? Can I bring him back again? I shall go to him, but he will not return to me."
>
> Then David consoled his wife Bathsheba, and went to her, and lay with her; and she bore a son, and he named him Solomon. (2 Samuel 12:18–24)

The story ends just like that. David washed, anointed himself, and changed his clothes. With one eye on his own death, he returned to the land of the living. Another son would be born, and that too would happen with grace.

You may feel that David didn't get what he deserved, that he got off too lightly; it seems to me otherwise. But it is indisputably true that God allowed him to get on with his life—the same chance, the same grace, he allows us all.

According to tradition, David composed a psalm, which I think reaches both the depths of humility and the heights of faith:

Do not remember the sins of my youth or my transgressions;
   according to your steadfast love remember me,
   for your goodness' sake, O LORD!
. . . .
For your name's sake, O LORD,
   pardon my guilt, for it is great.
Who are they that fear the LORD?
   He will teach them the way that they should choose.
They will abide in prosperity,
   and their children shall possess the land.
The friendship of the LORD is for those who fear him,
   and he makes his covenant known to them.
My eyes are ever toward the LORD,
   for he will pluck my feet out of the net.
Turn to me and be gracious to me,
   for I am lonely and afflicted.
Relieve the troubles of my heart,
   and bring me out of my distress.
Consider my affliction and my trouble,
   and forgive all my sins.

(Psalm 25:7, 11–18)

Now, don't imagine that grace will take care of *everything*. Even though God forgives, our loved ones do not forget. Things stay sticky for a while. Nor do second chances come cheaply, as we find when we confess to those we have wronged. Grace comes at a tremendous price. In the Christian sacrament of baptism, the ultimate form of confession and repentance, we are actually buried in the waters just as Christ was buried.

And that allows God to give us a new life.

—◊—

So this young man confronted by his fiancée found himself waist-deep in a disaster of his making. They were an exceptional couple in deciding to save what they could. He had realized—a little late, but after eight years with her, he had realized—how wonderful she was. He was determined to show her the difference, and she, much to her credit, was willing to see. I can't say that their relationship flourished right away, yet over many months they talked about things they had never discussed before, and while they still hadn't established full trust when they left my care, they were heading in that direction.

As I say, they were exceptional. Most folks instead choose to stay stuck in their problems. They're unwilling to take drastic solutions. But if you're going to "walk in newness of life," as Paul says, someone might have to cut the old clothes off you. And maybe something has to die—your pride, or your excuses, or your refusal to forgive. *You* have to die, in some sense. This is what we mean by dying and rising with Christ. It's not an abstract thing that happens outside your body. It really happens to you, and it hurts, and it feels wonderful, and it makes you free.

The wrong we do does not evaporate into thin air; and when it comes out, it's sticky, might be tracked all over town. We find it throughout the house, on doorknobs, on telephones, and on hot days long afterwards we can even smell it. Wallow in it if you like, but God's message has always been this:

Wash, change your clothes, get on with your life. Other voices may ring in your ears, but grace is sufficient—and God insists on having the last word.

Splitting the Atom

The world still seemed stable in the 1920s when scientists discovered its building blocks, subatomic particles—protons, electrons, and neutrons—and the force that binds them all together. The Nobel prize-winning chemist Francis Aston warned against "tinkering with the angry atom," but many scientists assumed that the binding forces could not be broken.

That's what Enrico Fermi assumed when he began bombarding the nuclei of atoms with neutrons. He tried this experiment on all the elements, until, at the very end of the periodic table, with the element uranium, he got a result he didn't expect and couldn't explain. It took a few years before he or anyone else realized that he had split the atom. Out of uranium he had created a new element, plutonium.

It was uncertain whether scientists could control a chain reaction, or whether, on a large scale, atoms would keep splitting indefinitely, unstoppably, until the world was destroyed.

Today we know that a chain reaction can happen in two ways: in bombs or in piles. In a bomb, the chain reaction is uncontrolled. It produces nothing but enormous destructive energy. In a carefully designed assembly that scientists call a "pile," the chain reaction is controlled, and it produces heat, or plutonium, or both. This is how nuclear power plants are run.

But on December 2, 1942, when Fermi's team of scientists gathered secretly beneath the football stadium at the University of

Chicago, where they had built a pile, they didn't know what would happen. They had made calculations on paper, but weren't sure whether their chain reaction could be controlled. Fermi flipped a switch, and a few minutes later he and his men rejoiced to find themselves still standing there.

Two-and-a-half years later, an uncontrolled reaction, that is, an atomic bomb, exploded over Japan. President Truman went on the radio to say:

> Sixteen hours ago an American airplane dropped one bomb on Hiroshima. . . . It is a harnessing of the basic power of the universe. The force from which the sun draws its power has been loosed against those who brought war to the Far East.[4]

As Christians, we believe that the basic power of the universe is something other than what scientists control. We believe that this force is love; that it comes from God, who gives it to us that the world might be blessed; and that, among all our gifts from God, the greatest of these is love.

But in human hands, the power of love can be dangerous and destructive. We all have seen this, and may even know it firsthand.

—〰—

The ancient Hebrews had rarely divorced, but by Jesus' day things were far more casual. Men could divorce women almost at whim, and in most places, though not in Palestine, women could divorce men just as easily. Divorce had become so common that some people chose not to marry. Does this sound familiar?

The Pharisees tried to trap Jesus on the issue, knowing that a soft line would anger many rabbis, while a hard line against divorce would make him unpopular with the people.

> Some Pharisees came, and to test him they asked, "Is it lawful for a man to divorce his wife?" He answered them, "What did Moses command you?" They said, "Moses allowed a man to write a certificate of dismissal and to divorce her." But Jesus said to them, "Because of your hardness of heart he wrote this

commandment for you. But from the beginning of creation, 'God made them male and female.' 'For this reason a man shall leave his father and mother and be joined to his wife, and the two shall become one flesh.' So they are no longer two, but one flesh. Therefore what God has joined together, let no one separate." (Mark 10:2–9)

Even in Jesus' day, this was a hard teaching. His audience must have squirmed as uncomfortably as we do. Yet there is something inescapably true about it.

In marriage we do become "one flesh," as Jesus said, we do surrender our separate selves to become one person, and this person has been given life by God. Before we kill it, we should think about the consequences.

Love is the basic power of the universe. We must not treat it casually.

—m—

At one time, the splitting of an atom worried us. We weren't so sure it could be controlled. As the world awaited nuclear war, the *Bulletin of Atomic Scientists* published a doomsday clock, indicating how close we were to midnight. Usually it was eleven o'clock.

But soon the power was controlled, and atoms were split for good, not evil, for medical treatments and electricity. The bombs were never used; the cold war ended; and soon we forgot our fear altogether.

In the same generation, we have come to believe that the splitting of marriages can accomplish good as well as evil. We have realized that some marriages are argumentative and abusive, and should be ended for the good of the children. We have forgotten the fear of divorce—the fear that it would produce a chain reaction throughout your life, your children's, and their children's.

Perhaps we have also forgotten that marriage involves the elemental power of the universe.

—m—

One morning not too long ago in upstate Michigan, two operators at the Big Rock nuclear power plant pushed two red buttons in the control room that took the steam turbines off-line and stopped the nuclear chain reaction. After thirty-five years, the Big Rock plant had shut down. It had been the oldest commercial nuclear plant in the United States.

In the weeks afterward, Consumers Power hired dozens of people, because it takes more people to shut down a nuclear plant than to run it. The company now had five years to dismantle the site and return it to a natural state. What would become of those six hundred acres on Lake Michigan? Would they become a state park? a marina? Well, they wouldn't be anything until they were rid of the radiation. And getting rid of it wasn't easy.

First, the fuel rods had to be removed from the reactor core. Eighty-two came out without accident, and then two got stuck. For ten anxious days this area waited to hear that they had been lifted safely.

Work moved to the "hazard reduction" phase: the removal of asbestos and so forth. A company called PN Services conducted an acid flush of the reactor pipes; filters soaked up the radiation, and then were shipped to Barnwell, South Carolina. They will be radio-active for a quarter of a million years.

It's much the same at the end of a marriage. We may rejoice that a bad marriage has ended, that a wronged spouse and impressionable children have been freed from an unhealthy situation; the atom has been split for good, not evil, but still there is this fallout that lingers for years.

What you get when you split the atom is a new element. You are never the same person you were before the marriage. You have become plutonium.

And even though your life has improved, it has not necessarily gotten easier.

—꿍—

As you may know, some states are concerned enough about the fallout from divorce that they are doing something about it. Couples in Louisiana are now offered a choice: they can apply for either a regular marriage license, which allows for no-fault divorce, or they can apply for a covenant marriage license. A declaration of intent for a covenant marriage license requires serious premarital counseling.

This covenant still allows for divorce on reasonable grounds—just not any grounds. It's a tall order—it's not for everybody—but it's closer to what Jesus described as a marriage.

I do not believe that Jesus would want us to continue in marriages that are broken beyond repair. I do not believe that he would want us to waste our lives, our spirits, in marriages that are abusive.

But I do believe that a marriage is a living thing that has been given life by God. Two people have been joined in "one flesh," animated by God's own spirit; and if we take its life, we do so at great peril.

For a generation now, we have forgotten the fear of the splitting atom and the splitting home. It is time for us to recover that fear. Before we do anything we might regret, before we do any lasting harm, let us honor the nuclear family and the power that holds it together.

Peshtigo

*P*eshtigo, Wisconsin, was a town of two thousand people. Along its sawdust streets and pine sidewalks, business was booming, big lumber business in the North Woods.

Each day the Peshtigo Lumber Company turned out hundreds of pails, tubs, fish kits, broom handles, clothespins, shingles, barrelheads, infant tubs called keelers, and buckets called kannikins. The lumber mill was also among the largest in the state.

The Peshtigo River carried these products to the Green Bay of Lake Michigan, where it was shipped down to Chicago. Soon there would be a rail connection to Chicago, for the Chicago & North Western was cutting down cedar, spruce, pine, and tamarack along the route, stacking the wood into great piles and setting them on fire.

Sunday, October 8, 1871, just after morning mass, Father Pernin of the Catholic Church noticed that there was no sun, just a strange yellow light. Birds were gathering and flying off, and he could hear a low, distant rumble. That evening he dug a trench in the yard of the rectory, put his trunk, his books, and church ornaments in it, and covered it with dirt. Then he put the tabernacle containing the sanctified elements of the Eucharist into his wagon.

About nine o'clock, a deer wandered into the middle of town, right into a pack of whimpering dogs. Without warning, a ball of fire fell right in the main street. Another fell, and then another, and the sawdust ignited. Townspeople fled the streets; some forty of

them fled into the lumber company's wood-frame boardinghouse.

One man saw young Helga Rockstad running down a sidewalk, her long blonde hair aflame. The next day all they found of her was her garter buckles and a mound of gray ash.

Many townspeople headed for the river. Father Pernin was driving there when a blast of hot wind knocked his buggy over. He left the wagon and the holy tabernacle and jumped into the river, which already was hot.

Peshtigo was burning on both sides of the river. One great crowd fled to the bridge and met people coming from the other side, so that people, horses, cows, and wagons all crowded at the middle as the bridge began to burn; and then it collapsed, tumbling men, women, and children into the water. Those who survived found themselves in new danger, as great flames reached out from the banks and set heads on fire.

Now the lumbermill went up in flames, and logs from the millpond caught fire and broke free, floating upriver into the crowds of survivors. Father Pernin saw a cow swimming through these flames—and stranger yet, Mrs. Heidenworth hanging for dear life onto one of its horns. The Peshtigo Company factory went up in a deafening explosion. Then a meteor shower of fiery tubs and buckets, keelers and kannikins, rained down on the people.

People who had jumped into wells suffocated. Axes and wedding rings melted. Crown fires leapt across the treetops, enormous balls of flame exploding hundreds of feet in the air. The winds were now at such a hurricane force that these fires carried all the way across the Green Bay and burned the Door County peninsula.

Six hundred people died in Peshtigo that night. Two hundred and thirty-five people died in the Sugar Bush settlements just outside of town, seventy-five on the peninsula, and at nearby Birch Creek, Michigan, twenty-two. Perhaps another two hundred died in isolated homesteads and logging camps. At the very minimum, 1,152 people died in this, the deadliest fire in North American history, and perhaps in all the world.

But the world at large took no notice—and to this day, many people do not know of it, for that same night, October 8, 1871, was the night of the Great Chicago Fire. People all around the world knew about Chicago, but few people have ever heard about Peshtigo.

—⚍—

Maybe your kids are in trouble. Maybe money is tight, or you've got a cold you can't shake, or a more serious illness that seems small compared to someone else's.

As a pastor, I hear people every day say, "Other people have it worse than me." Or, "I look at other people and realize I've got it pretty good." They look at a prayer list, see people suffering heart trouble, cancer, or a death in the family, and feel they have no right to worry about themselves.

There's a word for this: *Peshtigo.*

God never diminishes our troubles or suggests they are too little for him. Very much to the opposite, he pays strict attention.

Hagar, a minor character of the Old Testament, might well have figured that her problems didn't matter to God. After all, God's promises had been given to Abraham and Sarah, not her; she was their slave. God had promised them children without number, but when Sarah grew old and despaired of producing a child, she invited her husband to sleep with Hagar, thinking that the child would become their property. No sooner did Hagar conceive than Sarah grew jealous and beat her terribly. Hagar fled into the desert wilderness.

Poor, pregnant, and all alone, she came to a spring in the middle of nowhere. God, who knows everything, pursued her and spoke through an angel.

"Hagar, slave-girl of Sarah, where have you come from and where are you going?" the angel asked.

She said, "I am running away from my mistress Sarah."

The angel told her to go back, and made the very same promise to her that God had made to Abraham: descendants too many to count. "Now you have conceived and shall bear a son," the angel told her. "You shall call him Ishmael (which means God hears), for the Lord has given heed to your affliction."

At which she spoke these wonderful words: "You are a God of seeing" (Genesis 16:13).

—w—

Everybody knows about the Great Chicago Fire. It instantly became part of American folklore, and within days, people around the country were talking about Mrs. O'Leary's fabled cow.

But even though five times as many people died in Peshtigo that same night, hardly anybody knew about it—and how could they? It was in a remote area, and the telegraph wires had burned down. Only in November did belated accounts begin to appear in the national press, often buried beneath stories about Chicago. And there were no stories yet about another fire that happened that same Sunday night, October 8, 1871, this one in Michigan—even though this fire had consumed three times as much timberland as the tremendous fire in Peshtigo.

Starting first on the west shore of the Lower Peninsula, the fire had traveled across the state and wiped out towns from Port Huron to the top of the Thumb, continued along the Au Sable River, and into the Thunder Bay region.

At Holland, George Howard had sensed danger and handed out shovels to fourteen men who were standing around, but they had refused to work. It was the Sabbath day, they said. Thanks to another religious scruple, very few people in Holland had bought insurance, so the devastation to the town was a total loss.

At Forestville, John and Mary Kent fought the fire while their two daughters stayed in the house, but fires came up unseen and engulfed the house before the girls could be saved. John and Mary had to leave them there, driving away to the sound of their screams.

Two miles from the fire, entire fields of corn and potatoes were roasted in the ground; farther away, apple and peach trees broke out in untimely blossoms.

On that evil Sunday, October 8, 1871, Michigan lost two-and-a-half-million acres of woodland and more lives than were ever properly counted.

—⚏—

At times it seems no one knows or cares about our private disasters. Even in a small, close-knit church family, many needs go unnoticed. Some of your darkest nights may be your loneliest, because your close friends cannot read your mind. You may even say, "I don't need the special attention. Other people have it worse than me."

That's *Peshtigo*.

God would never diminish your need. Are you worried about something? This is what Jesus took to the cross: your trouble, *your trouble*.

Every concern that people brought to Jesus was important to him. He was not too great for anyone, nor was any trouble too small. According to him, God's concern is as minute as the sparrows, as immediate as the hairs on your head. Jesus told us this plainly, for the darkest times: "What I tell you in the dark, [proclaim] in the light" (Matthew 10:27 RSV). If something is important to you, it is important to God.

We can be slow to believe this. It took Hagar a second time to learn that God is a God of seeing.

As soon as Abraham and Sarah were blessed with a son of their own, Sarah regretted the other child she had willed into being, and once she saw Isaac and Ishmael playing together, she went a little crazy and demanded that Abraham send Hagar and her son away. Abraham was grieved; Ishmael was his son too. But early one morning, he gave Hagar a little bread and a skin of water and sent them away.

Once again she wandered in a desert wilderness. The water in the skin ran out. Death staring her in the face, she laid her son in the shade of a bush, and went a little farther where she would not have to watch him die. She lifted up her voice and wept.

Even there, in that lonely desert waste, God heard—heard not only her adult cries, but those of the child:

> God heard the voice of the boy; and the angel of God called to Hagar from heaven, and said to her, "What troubles you, Hagar? Do not be afraid; for God has heard the voice of the boy where he is. Come, lift up the boy and hold him fast with your hand, for I will make a great nation of him." Then God opened her eyes and she saw a well of water. (Genesis 21:17–19)

Moreover, "God was with the boy," and Ishmael grew to be a strong, capable young man, the father of a multitude. Of Hagar the story says no more. Perhaps she vanished into complete obscurity. Whatever became of her, no doubt someone saw to her needs— God be praised.

—ᨏᨎ—

It is impossible for even the most isolated needs to remain secret. Soon after the fire in Peshtigo, wagonloads of supplies arrived from Madison, Wisconsin. And many weeks later, *Harper's Weekly* printed a belated account, and help came in from all over the country. A church in Vermont, for example, sent $500 and twenty-five boxes of clothing.

No one thought to diminish the enormous loss by suggesting that Chicago should have more attention.

And even in the midst of tragedies were signs of God's concern. The morning after the fire, Father Pernin had come out of the river and found his wagon. The fire had burned a circle around it, but had left it—and the tabernacle containing the sanctified Eucharist—completely untouched. Not a scratch or a burn. To this day, the tabernacle sits in a museum in Peshtigo.

And in western Michigan, a sawmill operator, a huge and rough man, had seen the fire approaching his mill, and no end of efforts by his crew had seemed to stem it. At the last the mill operator had sworn a rude oath against God for allowing his property to go up in flames for no good reason, and he had told his men, "Go home, go home. Nothing more can be done. God can do as he damn well pleases."

At that moment a few drops of rain had fallen. Soon a heavy rain came down, as did his tears. He fell to the ground and said simply, "God be praised!"

Small comfort in such tragedy? Perhaps—but not to those weary men.

Your need is never small. There is no such thing with God. If it is important to you, it is important to him.

Jesus, who saw the worst and the best of life, speaks to us when we are alone in the terrible dark, when our hearts are aflame. He says, "God knows—and God cares. What I tell you in the dark, proclaim in the light!"

Let us fall to our knees and say, "God be praised!"

The I.G.A.

*I*n many small towns there is an I.G.A. In most I.G.A.s you can find dish soap, cream of chicken soup, saltines, and ground pork. You probably won't find sun-dried tomatoes, but you will find your next-door neighbor, and the clerk probably knows your name.

The big anonymous grocery chains sound like they involve real people—Sam's Club—while the Independent Grocers' Association sounds anonymous, even though its employees are your good friends. Wendy Poll at my hometown I.G.A. has been working there for fifteen years, putting in fifty to sixty hours a week, sometimes in the checkout line but usually ordering the food and stocking the shelves. Altogether the I.G.A. employs twenty people. Deliveries come from Alpena once a week, maybe twice in the summer.

Now, this is what you'll find in aisle two: chips, cereal, baking goods, bottled juice, canned fruit and vegetables, soups, Jell-O, dried milk, greeting cards, and the coffee grinder. There is no aisle eight. There is no aisle seven. There are only five aisles. If they don't have it, maybe you don't need it that badly.

Consider a can of I.G.A. brand stewed tomatoes. The label, it's fair to say, doesn't leap out and grab you. It doesn't beg you to buy it. It simply tells you what's inside the can. If you were already planning on buying some stewed tomatoes, you would find that these are the cheapest.

The Independent Grocers' Association began in 1926 as a way for small grocers to compete with the big chains. Over the years,

51

the chains have gotten bigger, while the I.G.A. has stubbornly remained simple and independent.

God bless this simplicity. Simplicity is true independence. God bless the good old I.G.A.

—៣—

We live in a land of plenty. That really is what we celebrate on Independence Day, our enormous plenty, our independence not only from England but from the conditions known by all the rest of the world through all of history. We, on the gaudy, glutted summit of our plenty, fire off thousands of dollars' worth of ephemeral fires—we literally burn money.

But are we really so free as we think? We have come to confuse plenty with independence, when for most of human life, independence has come through simplicity.

Jesus lived and taught a simple life. Like his teacher John the Baptist, he did not concern himself with getting or spending. He talked a lot about money, but only to say that it was a trap, that wealth was not the way to win release, liberation, independence, the new life.

In this, he reclaimed the ancient heritage of the nation Israel, which had been founded in simplicity for the betterment of all nations. You will recall that on their way to the promised land, the Hebrews had wandered in the desert, subsisting on crumbs of manna and small quail. Only after many years of this bare existence did they enter a rich land "flowing with milk and honey," and when they did, God made it clear to them that they should remember their humble beginnings. The simplicity, not the wealth, was to be their heritage. God even put this lesson in a song:

> "Now therefore write this song, and teach it to the Israelites; put it in their mouths, in order that this song may be a witness for me against the Israelites. For when I have brought them into the land flowing with milk and honey, which I promised on oath to their ancestors, and they have eaten their fill and grown fat, they will turn to other gods and serve them, despising me and

breaking my covenant. And when many terrible troubles come upon them, this song will confront them as a witness, because it will not be lost from the mouths of their descendants. For I know what they are inclined to do even now, before I have brought them into the land that I promised them on oath." That very day Moses wrote this song and taught it to the Israelites. (Deuteronomy 31:19–22)

Our own nation was founded by religious immigrants who withstood severe deprivations. They came at first not for material gain, but religious independence, and in the Shaker hymn "Simple Gifts" they expressed their belief that simplicity is true independence:

> *'Tis the gift to be simple, 'tis the gift to be free,*
> *'tis the gift to come down where we ought to be;*
> *and when we find ourselves in the place just right,*
> *'twill be in the valley of love and delight.*

—〰〰—

It is a point of pride with Americans that we have more than we need, and then some, and then some after that. That is why we demand so many products from which to choose. At a big supermarket up here, for example, in aisle two, all you'll find is cereal and juice. Aisle six is nothing but greeting cards. There are twenty aisles in all, plus a video store.

And then there's a chain of enormous groceries famous for having everything, including gas stations. They call it "one-stop shopping," but this is a misnomer. You stop several times, all in one store. You can't go in just for a can of stewed tomatoes—you go in *expecting* to buy things you hadn't planned on.

Israel, too, was "a land flowing with milk and honey," and the people grew rich and fat and happy, forgetful of their purpose and witness, until the Babylonians came and conquered them, and they lost everything—lost their land, lost their independence, and were carried into exile in Babylon, where even religious freedom was in jeopardy.

They lost everything, but they did regain their purpose. Once they had been merely Israelites, defined by their land. Now, in their exile, they were Jews, defined by their relationship with God. It is this purpose, this witness, which has withstood every loss, every deprivation, of the last twenty-six hundred years.

The American economy is built on keeping up with our neighbors, owning every little thing that they own. We even joke about it, saying when we spend too much, "Well, I'm doing my part for the economy."

The religious economy is built on something different. It is built on deliberately foregoing much that your neighbors have, because you sense that there is something else more valuable.

In it you are consciously modest about your material needs— and not merely because you wish to give to folks in need, and not merely because you have been commanded by Christ to feed the hungry, clothe the naked, and care for the sick. You do this because you know—you know in your soul—that the things you own own *you*—and you want to declare your independence.

—ɱ—

Rube Hildebrand came here as a young boy and worked for a few grocers before opening Hildebrand's Cash-and-Carry Grocery in 1915. In 1929, when the Depression hit, he went broke. But he refused to declare bankruptcy. Even though it took him many years, he paid off his debts to wholesalers.

Soon he started up a new grocery. In a few years he took over a small store on the south side of Main Street, and finally moved across the street to a larger place fifteen by twenty feet. Imagine this—*everything fit in there!* Not fourteen aisles, not even four aisles, but everything fit in there!

Like other grocers then, he offered credit. Sometimes Mae Hildebrand would say, "Now, Reuben, these folks are way behind— don't give them any more." And he'd say, "Mae—they've got five hungry kids to feed." They went on like that until 1943, when they sold out.

In those days there was more than just one grocery in town. There was Wager's Meat Market, Alden Founce's Harbor Springs

Grocery, an A&P on Main Street, Allerding's store just east of the gas station, Stanley Allen's grocery on Snyder Street, and the little East End Market.

Fifty years ago, a five-pound box of shrimp at the A&P cost $2.49. About that time things changed, the mom-and-pop groceries closed up, and the I.G.A. came in. Longtimers miss the many groceries, yet it's clear that their values have not been forgotten.

Wendy Poll of the Harbor I.G.A. learned the business from her grandfather, Carl Poll. He still owns the place, and his son, Carl Jr., and grandson, Carl III, help to run it. They have to keep prices down to stay competitive. It's tough to stay in business with the big chains, Wendy says. They try to know most of their customers by their names, ask about their families. And believe it or not, they still make deliveries, which older folks appreciate.

True, you probably won't find lemon-pepper linguine. But God bless the I.G.A.

—m—

God bless the U.S.A. For several generations now, our country has been preoccupied with money. Folks who lived through the Depression have been obsessed with saving it. Baby boomers have been obsessed with spending it. Perhaps another generation will remember the song taught us long years ago by countrymen and -women who believed that simplicity is true independence.

You already know this song—and perhaps your children will sing it back to you:

> *'Tis the gift to be simple, 'tis the gift to be free,*
> *'tis the gift to come down where we ought to be;*
> *and when we find ourselves in the place just right,*
> *'twill be in the valley of love and delight.*
>
> *When true simplicity is gained,*
> *to bow and to bend we shan't be ashamed.*
> *To turn, turn, will be our delight,*
> *'till by turning, turning, we come round right.*

It Puts Food on the Table

As a new pastor just out of seminary, I looked like I'd been fed on shadows and skim water. Well, that was one condition a Methodist church could remedy. In short order I gained ten pounds just by visiting parishioners such as Deyo and LaVon Beall.

They lived in a retirement home, and when I came, they always set out some storebought cookies and weak tea. Deyo was eighty-five, totally bald, his body now shaped to his wheelchair. Twenty-four hours a day, he relied on an oxygen tank. It allowed him a few words or bursts of laughter. He had a fierce look but a gentle manner, and his narrow eyes fastened on me like a hawk's even when he said the nicest things.

One afternoon, that first year that we knew each other, Deyo, LaVon, and I were playing pinochle as the oxygen hose kept slipping from his nose. He was telling me about the farm he had bought for her—about how he had bought it at first sight, without her knowledge. He described how they had moved out there while the farmhouse was still occupied by pigs; she told me how he had dug three ponds and stocked them with swans, and named one of the swans after her.

All this storytelling tired him out. He coughed and asked, "Are you hungry?" I said sure. So we had dinner that night in the retirement home. I don't remember much of what we ate except that everything was boiled or steamed.

He watched me closely. He wanted me to tell a story. At last he asked, Why did I become a pastor?

I told him only part of the story of my call—it's not a story that I can tell everybody. I shared with him about the college professor who had encouraged me to consider it, about my hesitations—and even though I withheld the heart of the matter, I did want him to know that I found the work significant and rewarding.

After the dessert—I think it was boiled egg custard—he asked, "Did you get enough to eat?" And I felt very nourished. This, this very moment, was the reason I became a pastor.

—⁓—

We are all called to do the work of Christ: to serve our neighbors and proclaim the gospel through our deeds. Some people hear this call, and their lives are changed by it.

We're all called, and yet, for better or worse, the Christian life is usually symbolized by pastors. Doubtless the people who most regret this are pastors, and still they take on the day-to-day responsibilities; the business and the dreaming; the little and the large tasks of church families.

Today the church faces a clergy shortage, and within that a shortage of excellence. Many pastors will retire in the next few years; the gifts and graces of those who will remain vary widely. For several generations now, our finest youth, even those active in church, have rarely chosen Christian ministry—and who can blame them? They have not heard the call. No one is encouraging them. God's call is too gentle and soft to be heard within our deafening silence.

Paul found great joy in God's service. Despite all his hardships, he relished the calling. In First and Second Timothy and Titus, the so-called "pastoral letters," he instructed the next generation to be diligent, to be modest, to serve gladly.

Second Timothy is perhaps the most personal of all his letters. We get a glimpse into his heart, into his deepest satisfactions:

In the presence of God and of Christ Jesus, who is to judge the living and the dead, and in view of his appearing and his kingdom, I solemnly urge you: proclaim the message; be persistent whether the time is favorable or unfavorable; convince, rebuke, and encourage, with the utmost patience in teaching. For the time is coming when people will not put up with sound doctrine, but having itching ears, they will accumulate for themselves teachers to suit their own desires, and will turn away from listening to the truth and wander away to myths. As for you, always be sober, endure suffering, do the work of an evangelist, carry out your ministry fully.

As for me, I am already being poured out as a libation, and the time of my departure has come. I have fought the good fight, I have finished the race, I have kept the faith. From now on there is reserved for me the crown of righteousness, which the Lord, the righteous judge, will give me on that day, and not only to me but to all who have longed for his appearing. (2 Timothy 4:1–8)

If I, like Paul, am speaking to another generation, I would hope to find words adequate to say that pastoring really is wonderful. It is honest. It is meaningful. It is joyful. It is humane. It is divine. And you know, it puts food on the table.

Of course, it's not the easiest life.

You have to be able to keep many priorities simultaneously— you are, as one pastor says, "a stray dog at a whistlers' convention."

The hours are very long, and if you are at all human and conscientious, work will crawl into bed with you.

You have to bury your friends.

If you are married, your spouse must be understanding and durable.

The pay is low, because folks want to make sure you're not in it for the money.

Against all odds, you must maintain an authentic faith life.

That said, it is good work, and it puts food on the table—not just yours, but on the holy table where others are fed. This is a hungry world, and that's what makes the pastorate such a demanding, rewarding, and essential life.

—⟋⟋⟍—

LaVon cared for Deyo, checked his oxygen, gave him his pills, and when things got to be too much, took on a visiting nurse. It worried her sick. Their relaxation was to sit down for a game of cards.

When Deyo was eighty-six, LaVon died. He had never imagined that she might go first. As the force of his mind gave way to grief, those narrow eyes shed such tears; he lost his appetite and sat by the window, choking back his self-pity but unable to find anything else to discuss.

Once he set his sharp gaze on me and asked, "Why do you spend so much time with an old man like me?"

How could I explain to him how wonderful he was even in the broken-down end of his life? So I said, "Tell me about the swan named LaVon."

—⟋⟋⟍—

It is a hungry world. There is a good reason that God has sustained the church through all its years of failure and neglect, why God has called pastors when no one else has called them: the world is hungry, and the Word is food.

It is why we gather at this table for Holy Communion. We all need to be fed in ways that transcend worldly appetites. The very fact of our own need calls us into some kind of Christian service.

God's call is gentle and soft, so soft that it may need human voices to join in chorus. If you have ever been hungry—materially, spiritually—then you should give voice to the call for those who might feed you.

I took Communion to Deyo one day when he was eighty-seven. He told me about the swans again (he said the one named LaVon had a bad disposition), and I could tell him the full story of my call. He was not offended, and I hope you will not be, either.

—⁓—

When I went off to college I had no use for church whatsoever. My family had occasionally attended a Methodist church of blue-haired ladies and turgid music, and what little I had learned there seemed to me very useless, unbelievable, or mildly offensive.

But then I got to know Dr. Edmund Perry, a professor who often took lunch in my dining hall. Everyone knew him; he was a legend on campus. A onetime country pastor, he was now the chairman of the religion department and author of some important work on Christianity and Buddhism. He had white hair, a crooked, rakish smile, and a Georgian accent, and he loved to scandalize us by asking intimate questions with perfect Southern charm. Yet he could also be proud and imposing, as when, on my first day in his New Testament class, he introduced students who had been named after him by their parents.

One day at lunch he said to several of us, "You don't get meals here on Sunday, do you?" No, we said. "Well, Mrs. Perry and I would be delighted to have you over for Sunday dinner, if you'd join us for church in the morning."

It seemed a small price to pay for a home-cooked meal. So despite my agnosticism I trudged over to the First United Methodist Church and sat with the Perrys in the balcony.

Well, it wasn't half bad. The large, historic sanctuary and full choir surpassed what I had known back home. People of all ages and backgrounds, people who ordinarily wouldn't have anything to do with each other, worshiped together. To my amazement I found that church people were real people—humane and open-minded, comfortable with doubt. The difference, I'm now sure, wasn't in the place, but in me; and very soon college would so humble me that the unmerited love of God and the grace of Christ would become quite real to me. The Perrys never pressed the point, but I went to church with them now and again, until I attended regularly on my own. During my undergraduate years God became real to me, and quietly I became a Christian.

It never occurred to me where such a change in life might lead. To many friends I was a counselor, and some thought I should become a psychologist, but I wanted to write and perhaps teach. I did help out around the church office and led a group for young adults. But my plans were the same as before.

One Sunday in my senior year, while Mrs. Perry was clearing away the dishes from her table—she had fixed "sunshine chicken," as I recall—Dr. Perry put down his coffee, pushed away from his place, and asked, "Larry, when are you going to become a Methodist minister?"

I shook my head and laughed, but Dr. Perry held my gaze, speaking seriously and intently.

"Larry," he said, "the Methodist Church needs pastors with *balls.*"

And that is the story of my call. I became a pastor because someone cared enough to ask me, and to put it in the most blunt and urgent words.

Why did I become a pastor? Because of you, Deyo. I trust that you are listening today. I hope that you and LaVon are enjoying a game of pinochle, and I hope that you know that a life has been touched by yours. Help me today, I pray.

Fall

The Peaceable Kingdom

*I*n Philadelphia, the city of brotherly love, stands the Friends Meeting Hall, the largest and most historic Quaker house of worship. Here, a hundred and seventy years ago, a man named Edward Hicks attended the Yearly Meeting of Friends, or Quakers, who had come from all over the young United States. Remarkably, he was known as a preacher, even though preaching was not common among Quakers. He was also a painter, when painting among them was even more rare.

Since his boyhood he had decorated coaches and milk cans and rugs and signs, and now, in his middle age, he had begun painting canvasses—copy after copy of the same work, called *The Peaceable Kingdom*. It is an allegory of Isaiah 11:6:

> *The wolf shall live with the lamb,*
> *the leopard shall lie down with the kid,*
> *and the calf and the lion together,*
> *and a little child shall lead them.*

In this version, you can see the calf and the lion prominently; the wolf and the lamb at the far right, the leopard and the kid below them, and they are indeed led by a little child, actually several children.

In the left background of the picture is another scene—not biblical, though deeply meaningful to Hicks and his vision of America. It shows William Penn, the founder of the Pennsylvania colony, concluding a treaty with the Delaware Indians. Penn, a Quaker, paid the Indians for their land and wrote rules for their fair treatment; he wanted no war, no violence of any kind. This was

perhaps the only treaty between Indians and Christians that was never broken. Penn told the Indian chief, "All will be brotherhood and love. I consider us the same flesh and blood joined by one heart." And the chief reportedly said, "The Indians and colonists must live in love as long as the sun and moon give light."

In those years, many people believed that the United States could be a place of peace and justice. For one of the few times in human history, it was possible to believe in a peaceable kingdom, in the words of Isaiah made manifest.

Edward Hicks never tired of this subject. He painted *The Peaceable Kingdom* a hundred times or more. His eternally youthful pictures hang in galleries all over our country, reminders of its early promise, and of the faith that shaped it.

I suppose we all want a world like this painting—not in childlike dreaming, but in truth, when all God's creatures will live within their differences. This is what many people mean by the kingdom of God.

The kingdom comes in fractions, in eighths and sixteenths and denominations, and it has always been so. Ever since the very start of Christianity, when Paul, Peter, and James worked out their differences, which were reflected in distinctive congregations, we have been inching along toward the will of God.

Not that that is a bad thing. Some Christians worry over our "divided witness," but I do not particularly regret it. It allows us to reach a greater variety of people. Nor are divisions unique to Christianity—every world religion has them; and in any event, ultimate unity is not ours; it is God's. We testify to, even if we do not manifest, a transcendent unity and peace.

What does bother me is when Christians *within* churches fight. It never happens over our missions or witness, but instead over petty or peripheral things. Friends stop speaking to each other, or speak bitterly. They may pretend to obey a shepherd, but tear at each other like lions or wolves.

Up where I live, a group opposed to renovating St. Francis Catholic Church has littered the county with big red signs that say *Preserve St. Francis* and filled the airwaves with calls to *Hold your money*! Worshipers have been horrified to find their church conflict on the front pages of the distant Detroit papers.

The children of St. Francis, meanwhile, just like children elsewhere, have led them. They're busy with missions work.

One of the great founders of our faith, the apostle Paul, was by nature defensive and combative, and we see from his own letters in the New Testament that trouble followed him everywhere. Yet over time he changed, and found peace as a servant of Christ. To the good people of Philippi, he could even say,

> Some proclaim Christ from envy and rivalry, but others from goodwill. These proclaim Christ out of love, knowing that I have been put here for the defense of the gospel; the others proclaim Christ out of selfish ambition, not sincerely but intending to increase my suffering in my imprisonment. What does it matter? Just this, that Christ is proclaimed in every way, whether out of false motives or true; and in that I rejoice. (Philippians 1:15–18)

This may have been the high-water mark of Paul's spiritual maturity. He wasn't just being magnanimous; no, he really had found peace by concentrating on his missions work. In this letter, he thanked the church at Philippi, which had shared most generously in that mission:

> Make my joy complete: be of the same mind, having the same love, being in full accord and of one mind. Do nothing from self-ish ambition or conceit, but in humility regard others as better than yourselves. Let each of you look not to your own interests, but to the interests of others. Let the same mind be in you that was in Christ Jesus, who, though he was in the form of God, did not regard equality with God as something to be exploited, but emptied himself, taking the form of a [servant]. (Philippians 2:2–7)

When we set our minds on the needs of others, it's impossible for us to be divided, and even in our churches the wolf and lamb, the calf and the lion, can lie down together.

—⁂—

In Philadelphia, the city of brotherly love, on North Fourth Street, is St. George's United Methodist Church, the world's oldest Methodist church in continuous use.

When it became a Methodist church in 1769, it followed the way of William Penn, and practiced religious and racial toler-ance—or toleration. Blacks were allowed to worship there. In fact, the congregation boasted the first black man licensed to preach in Methodism, Richard Allen. But that did not mean that all races worshiped together. No, Richard Allen led services for blacks at five o'clock in the morning.

This arrangement held until one Sunday in 1787, when whites told blacks that they could use only the balcony. Allen was out-raged. He soon led his congregation out and founded the African Methodist Episcopal Church, which continues to this day.

St. George's is a historic spot, though I suspect that it would pre-fer a different history in the city of brotherly love.

Not far from there, at 320 Arch Street, between Third and Fourth Streets, is the Friends Meeting Hall. Here Edward Hicks attended a meeting of Quakers that ended in a schism between orthodox believers and his cousin, Elias Hicks. The orthodox accused Hicks of too liberal a theology, while he accused them of elevating Scripture above the Spirit which had inspired it. He also felt that they had failed to boycott the products of slave labor.

Elias belonged to the tradition of moderate Quakers, such as William Penn and George Washington. Now, in 1827, feeling no longer at home in the denomination, Hicksites walked out of the yearly meeting, and reluctantly Edward Hicks followed his fire-brand cousin.

But the schism bothered him deeply. For another twenty years, he continued to paint *The Peaceable Kingdom* as he mourned the split among the Quakers. Obsessively he painted the same sub-ject—the calf and the lion, the wolf and the lamb, the little child—and while none of his canvasses was quite perfect, many of them were very fine. Out of more than a hundred, only fifty or so survive.

—⁓—

We have made hundreds of attempts to render the peaceable king-dom. None of them has been quite perfect, although some have been quite fine. We seem never to tire of the subject. We still believe that lions and lambs can lie down together.

I'm thinking of two congregations near my home, in neighbor-ing small towns, churches that sapped each other's strength for generations. Neither one ever got big enough to do much, or wanted anything to do with the other. When the children came together, though, they had a great time and said so to their parents.

At last the congregations settled their rivalry and merged. They were briefly divided as to where they would worship: both factions wanted their church building. With considerable prayer they decided to build a new place out in the country that would serve not only their needs, but those of the area—and, I'm glad to say, the first thing they put in the blueprint was a food pantry.

They built on farmland with views of the wide fields and quiet pines and a creek, and right away felt at home. One of the first worship services there was a funeral for an outdoorsman. Three deer came up to the big window behind the altar and looked in on the proceedings. A doe and two fawns pressed their noses to the glass. The people in the pews were startled and deeply moved.

The kingdom comes in fractions, but it comes. God's will is done on earth when his people set their minds on the needs of others. That's all it takes to provide a meetinghouse of friends.

Little Blue Books

Some years ago when I was ordained, a family member gave me some well-worn booklets from the 1920s. Little Blue Book number 1484 was titled *Why Preachers Go Bad*. Not your typical ordination gift! Number 936 offered *A Logical Objection to Christianity,* while number 1084 asked, *Did Jesus Ever Live?*

They had been published in, of all places, Girard, Kansas. I figured there had to be a story behind them, and sure enough, there was.

In the 1920s, when all the world was being shocked by sex and jazz, the firm of Haldeman-Julius made a name for itself publishing cheap editions of the classic and controversial Little Blue Books on politics, sex education, and religion. Eventually it sold six thousand titles through the mail—some of them written by E. Haldeman-Julius himself. A committed atheist, he authored *The Meaning of Atheism* and *The Church Is a Burden, Not a Benefit, in Social Life.* As far as he was concerned, all Christians were like the Pentecostals who surrounded him on the prairie.

By contrast, he would be the most modern of men. He had little love or use for Girard, preferring New York City and going there often for business and recreation. He could afford to do so. E. Haldeman-Julius (he rarely used his first name) had become a minor celebrity—the Book Baron, the Ford of Literature, the Barnum of Books. In New York he sat in on the legendary Algonquin Round Table of Dorothy Parker, Robert Benchley, George S.

Kaufman, and the Marx brothers, a bright and successful man who had no use for something as dull as a faith.

—⚹—

The Spirit moves where it will, among whom it chooses. I don't know why some people respond to it while others seem unaware of it. Some of the smartest and most accomplished people miss it entirely. Some of the least promising people know it intimately. I don't know what the difference is, but for want of anything better, I will call it the religious imagination.

Some people have the imagination to see God at work in the world—in the variety and comedy and tragedy of life and death, the music of coincidence, the poetry of unexpected love. They delight in life's patterns, and feel grief without being destroyed by it. These people can receive the Spirit of God.

Others may be tremendously creative, but lacking the religious imagination, they do not know when the Spirit of God blows over and through them.

Why do some people have a religious imagination while others do not? Perhaps it is predestined. John Calvin thought so after reading the story of Jacob and Esau, the smart and foolish brothers. In the Book of Genesis, God says, "Jacob have I loved, and Esau have I hated." Calvin took this to mean that God favors some and not others, and predestines whether we will receive God's Spirit.

But there is another possibility, for the story of Pentecost suggests that the Spirit of God is for all. Thousands of Jews from dozens of countries had come to Jerusalem for the ancient festival, speaking many different languages—Parthians, Phrygians, Arabs, Cretans. Perhaps they understood the Hebrew that the priests spoke in the Temple; but who could understand them? In their several languages, they had to ask for lodging, food, currency exchange, medical assistance; and at every turn they were reminded that they were foreigners.

Christians, too, were gathered in Jerusalem for the Pentecost.

The Holy Spirit came upon them, and as we read in the Book of Acts, they were able to understand all languages. Unlikely people—foreigners—heard the gospel in their own tongues, received the Holy Spirit, and the church was born.

> When the day of Pentecost had come, they were all together in one place. And suddenly from heaven there came a sound like the rush of a violent wind, and it filled the entire house where they were sitting. Divided tongues, as of fire, appeared among them, and a tongue rested on each of them. All of them were filled with the Holy Spirit and began to speak in other languages as the Spirit gave them ability.
>
> Now there were devout Jews from every nation under heaven living in Jerusalem. And at this sound the crowd gathered and was bewildered, because each one heard them speaking in the native language of each. Amazed and astonished, they asked, "Are not all these who are speaking Galileans? And how is it that we hear, each of us, in our own native language?" (Acts 2:1–8)

The Holy Spirit is for us all. Perhaps we have not been born with a religious imagination, but the Spirit may blow over us and through us, and change all that.

Emanuel Julius was born July 30, 1889, to a family of Russian Jews. Both his grandfathers had been rabbis. His name, Emanuel, meant "God is with us." As an adult, he rarely used it, signing himself just *E*.

The family lived in a Philadelphia ghetto, where his father was a bookbinder. To escape their grinding poverty, Emanuel fled at age seventeen to New York City, and for the next ten years didn't contact his family. In 1925, at the height of his fame, he visited them for a few hours, and then never again, although he always wrote about them warmly.

In 1915 he came to Girard, Kansas, to work on the *Appeal to Reason,* the nation's largest Socialist newspaper, which had recently published *The Jungle* by Upton Sinclair. There he had tremendous good fortune.

First, the publisher committed suicide.

Then Julius married Marcet Haldeman, daughter of the richest man in town, and with her money he was able to buy the print shop. He joined his name to hers, becoming Haldeman-Julius.

That was about as far as their intimacy went. By all accounts he was not a pleasant person. He worked long hours and treated his employees brutally:

> He would fire you at the drop of a hat. With the stealth of a cat, he moved quietly about his plant, bounding up the front or the back stairs three at a time, always in a hurry or possibly hoping to catch a loafer off-guard. Leaning against the stair post, cigar in mouth, he would stand there, immobile, his piercing eyes sweeping over the entire floor, causing every girl to freeze in her tracks. One somehow got the feeling she had just been run through with a saber. . . . He would hurry into his office, slam the door, and sprawl out with *The Wall Street Journal* and *The New York Times.*[5]

His second wife recalls:

> He was not a family man to the extent that he wanted to share his evenings with them. . . . When Daddy drove into the driveway at five o'clock, all noise—like the children's phonograph—must cease and little playmates scatter for home. . . . He usually ate lunch alone in his library, which was off-limits to the rest of the family. . . . People were necessary accoutrements to him, but he enjoyed no one's company more than his own. . . . As he once wrote, "I am a little world all to myself."[6]

This former socialist took to driving a custom-built Lincoln coupe, black with orange disc wheels, and heading off for long weekends with female companions. He despised Girard, hated small-town Kansas life, and savored every occasion to see New York. He was in New York, actually on the floor of the Stock Exchange, the day of the crash that wiped out his fortune.

—⁓—

The Spirit of God waits for us.

Many of us write and publish our own Little Blue Books. We say things like, "God is all well and good, but I can't stand church." Or, "The Bible is really a book for children." Or, "We should separate the teachings of Jesus from the miracles." This says a lot about our imaginations. Fortunately the Spirit of God is upon us, waiting, waiting until we recognize its presence.

We sometimes think that Pentecost was a one-time-only wonder, a long-ago miracle that happened to a mere three thousand people. Well, it happens to millions of people; it happens today; it happens to *us* as we discover the sacredness of things we took for granted.

After the day of the Crash, Haldeman-Julius never saw New York again. He gave up his Lincoln, drove a modest Ford, and rarely left Kansas. The long hours he worked now were not to advocate his causes or to get rich, but to survive. He had made a lot of money, he had lost a lot of money; his six thousand books had not changed the world. Hundreds of thousands of Little Blue Books had made their way from Girard, Kansas—the very heart of the Bible Belt— to the sophisticated cities; still the cities continued to see the same numbers of people in worship. Girard, Kansas, also saw the usual numbers in worship, as if there were a universal rule that despite changes in intellectual fashion, a certain number of folks would always have the religious imagination.

The Spirit of God is upon us all—even on Haldeman-Julius, whose first name was Emanuel, *God is with us.*

After his first wife died in 1941, he married again, gave up other women, and made himself at home in Kansas, taking delight in the rural life that once had seemed small and charmless. He had not been an attentive father, but when he and his wife purchased an incubator, he threw himself into the project. He scoured the countryside for setting eggs, and talked of going into the chicken business.

Eventually, the red-letter day arrived for the chicks to start hatching. Excited as an expectant father, H-J spent most of his day in the hatching room waiting for the first yellow head to emerge limply from its shell. I had to reproach him for opening the incubator so much and allowing the eggs to chill. When at last he did find the first fluffy yellow chick standing bewildered in the tray, he stood there in total wonder as though a great miracle had taken place right before his eyes. Gathering the tiny thing gently into his cupped hands, like a happy child he proudly carried it into the plant for all his employees to see.[7]

He even became friends with a priest, who asked him what he got out of life. He said:

I find life worthwhile because I enjoy good music, great books, beautiful thoughts of truth and freedom, pleasant home life, exchange of ideas, black bread smeared with homemade butter, letters dictated by my grandchild, friendly neighbors, newborn calves, freshly plowed fields, burning logs that make the house smell sweet, my wife's lovely garden, the fields mantled in snow, soft-voiced old people, laughing children, the long yawn that says it's time to turn in.[8]

This is the religious imagination. This is part of God's sustaining grace—not full salvation, mind you, but close to it.

The Spirit of God is patient. It wants to speak to any of us. Then, on our own personal Pentecost, it blows over and through us, and changes how we look at our world. We must take nothing for granted, not one neighbor, not one worker, not one child, not one chick—for in such things the Holy Spirit is speaking our language.

Can you hear it?

Mr. Jefferson's Bible

*H*e was a democrat and an aristocrat; a conservative and a reformer; one of the leading botanists of his day, a great architect, an accomplished violinist, a student of philosophy and the physical sciences. His gift of ten thousand volumes from his own library established the Library of Congress, and he founded the University of Virginia. Yet this brilliant landed gentleman was haunted by a simple peasant. Thomas Jefferson said of Jesus:

> His parentage was obscure; his conditions poor; his education null; his natural endowments great; his life correct and innocent; he was meek, benevolent, patient, firm, disinterested, & of the most sublime eloquence.[9]

Jefferson had nothing but contempt, however, for the writers of the four Gospels:

> The committing to writing his life & doctrines fell on the most unlettered and ignorant men; who wrote, too, from memory, & not till long after the transactions had passed.[10]

For years, Thomas Jefferson dreamed of separating the authentic words and actions of Jesus, the holiness of Jesus, from what he imagined were the elaborations of the gospels. In 1803, soon after he had become our third president, he created his own New Testament. He sat down with two Bibles and a pair of scissors, cut out the passages he believed in, and pasted them into the pages of a blank book.

The virgin birth—gone. The miracles—gone. Christ's divinity—gone. The resurrection—gone.

He called this book *The Philosophy of Jesus,* and he read from it every night. It ran to all of forty-six pages.

—◊◊◊—

I caution us against judging Mr. Jefferson, because each of us has done exactly the same thing. Not with scissors and glue, perhaps—but we all have edited Bibles we can believe in. Whoever we are, whether we are traditional or unorthodox, we pick and choose among the passages for what makes us comfortable. We edit out the parts that are difficult, or obscure, or unlikely. We edit out the laws and the wars, leave out God's judgments of some people, or God's acceptance of others.

I think we miss the point.

The point of the Bible is that we cannot accept it easily. The point of the Bible is that it challenges us. The point of the Bible is that it is broader than our own experience, broader than our reason, broader than our most reckless dreaming, broader than anything else except the holy. If you think that your own mind encompasses everything that is holy, then perhaps you do not need the Bible.

But then again, perhaps you do.

—◊◊◊—

At the very end of the Gospel of John, after twenty-one chapters of teachings and miracles—indeed, at the very end of the four gospels—we read this passage:

> This is the disciple who is testifying to these things and has written them, and we know that his testimony is true. But there are also many other things that Jesus did; if every one of them were written down, I suppose that the world itself could not contain the books that would be written. (John 21:24–25)

The author of John was correct. At the time he wrote this, there were dozens of other gospels circulating, some that have been lost to us, and others that have survived—the Gospel of Thomas, the Gospel of Bartholomew, the Protevangelium of James, the Infancy Gospel of Thomas. There were so many gospels, of such varying authenticity, that the early church had to determine which should be given official approval. Over several decades, it set the canon of our New Testament. Yet what remained was anything but tidy.

The church quite deliberately chose not one gospel, but four. These differ significantly—at some points, they flatly contradict each other. You can also say they broaden each other.

For many of us, these discrepancies make the Bible more believable. The Bible does not try to hide them. It presents them candidly, as the wrinkles and beauty marks of an old and trusted friend. As the author of John said, there are so many things to be told, so many ways of telling them, that the whole world could not contain them all. Not only is holiness bigger than you or me—it is bigger than the Bible itself.

—◠◡◠—

And yet some folks are always trying to shrink the Bible.

There's a group of scholars—they call themselves the Jesus Seminar—who meet every year to decide which of Jesus' sayings and doings, as recorded in the New Testament, are authentic. A few years ago they announced that only 18 percent of the words attributed to Jesus were actually spoken by him. They were determined, just like Mr. Jefferson, to scrape off the crust and rediscover the historical Jesus.

Common to these searches for the historical Jesus is a presupposition that the Gospels were written by ignorant hacks, that they are mere propaganda and not true representations of Jesus' thought. I suspect otherwise. The Gospels are highly artful, brilliantly concise, fully human stories, which in their blend of faith and fact may be truer to Jesus than any modern revision could ever be.

The Jesus Seminar has produced its own Bible, called (rather smugly, I think) the Scholars Version. The words of Jesus are color-coded to indicate how the scholars voted on their authenticity. Like Mr. Jefferson's Bible, it dispenses with miracle stories. It adds the Gospel of Thomas, which has no miracle stories—only pithy little sayings that sound faintly Buddhist. This is, surely, a Bible for our times.

You read only the red or pink passages, and what you get is an egalitarian, anti-authoritarian Jesus, a Jesus with whom college professors can be comfortable. Soon they will release another Bible assessing which of Jesus' deeds actually happened. I can hardly wait!

Now there is one good thing to be said for these amputated Bibles. They might actually get used. Jefferson read his maimed Bible every night—and so do many of us use ours, rereading favorite passages we have highlighted. I would hope that as we get used to these maimed and disfigured Bibles, too weak to do us any harm, we might eventually want the full Bible, because we are ready to be challenged by it.

Perhaps it might even set us free of ourselves.

—⁓—

I myself don't find all scripture equally helpful, or feel that the Bible must be swallowed whole, like a horse pill. Great figures of the faith have also balked at some of it. Rabbis who fixed the canon of the Hebrew Bible had doubts about including Esther, Ecclesiastes, and the Song of Songs. The early Christian church fathers almost did away with the Hebrew Bible and several of Paul's letters. Martin Luther called the Letter of James "an epistle of straw," while the Swiss reformer Huldrych Zwingli dismissed the Book of Revelation as "not a biblical book. . . . It has no savor of the mouth or the mind of John. I can, if I so will, reject its testimonies." But in the end they accepted the variety and strangeness of scripture and were willing to reckon with passages that challenged them. They accepted the Bible's power to offend the prejudices of any person or era—because the holy is greater than the nice, the neat, the rational, or the fashionable.

In the Gospel of John, Jesus has these words for his disciples; I don't know if they should be printed in red, but I believe they are, in the most important sense, authentic:

> "If you continue in my word, you are truly my disciples; and you will know the truth, and the truth will make you free." (John 8:31–32)

It's ironic that Thomas Jefferson, a champion of liberty, remained a slaveholder all his life. He thought about freeing all his slaves, but at last freed only the slave children he had sired, and never was set free of himself. Perhaps that's why he snipped and snipped until he had a Jesus cut to his own idealized profile, his own silhouette. He did revise and expand his little Bible, but not with more passages, only with Greek, Latin, French, and English translations, arranged in four parallel columns. He called this book *The Life and Morals of Jesus of Nazareth.* He had set out to capture and distill what was holy, but right at the outset he had discarded much of its strangeness and power.

Here is the Bible we have been given. Maybe we think we enjoy a loftier perspective than the men and women who first read it, or that we have bigger minds and broader souls. Maybe we suppose we are bigger than the Bible and do not need all of it.

Then again, perhaps we do.

Farmer's Cheese

Summer is the tourist season in northern Indiana, Amish country. The buggies, the black hats, and the quilts are on display for the hundreds and thousands of tourists who fill small towns like Bremen, Goshen, and Nappanee. So many tourists have come to "get away from it all" that the highways are jammed, and you have to wait in line a long time to get fudge or ice cream, or shoofly pie.

The Amish seem to live a life apart. They live out of town, on farms without machinery, without telephone or television, attending their own schools, and, of course, keeping their own faith. Yet they do not hide from the world—out of their own homes they sell chicken, canned fruit, Swiss cheese, Muenster cheese, and a tasty variety with anise seeds and dill called farmer's cheese.

They do not hide from the world, and in fact certain lapsed Amish can be downright worldly, making a good living from their heritage. A gigantic restaurant called Das Dutchman Essenhaus, run by former Amish, serves thousands of farm suppers each night. Just down the road is an enormous resort complex called Amish Acres, where you can stay in something approaching luxury, tended by local Baptists and Methodists in Amish costume.

None of this will prepare you for the experience of Shipshewana, which on Tuesdays and Wednesdays becomes the world's largest flea market. You simply can't (and don't want to) imagine the sweaty press and the crass commerce, all the unnecessary items sold by folks once known for the simple life.

Across the road from Shipshewana is Menno-Hof, a museum of

the faith's past and present. Relics of the Mennonites and Amish are kept under glass, and a tour guide will tell you about their theology. It is a quiet, thoughtful place. But back out on the main street are tourist shops, T-shirt shops, and trinket shops, all of which are, frankly, cheesy.

—∞—

The apostle Paul warned us that our faith was different from the world around us, that we would be tempted to give it up, and he has been proved right in every generation. As millions of Christians know by now, the Christian faith is difficult. So we make compromises—accommodating to the opinions of others, changing our ways, carrying the gospel behind pursed lips.

Our faith has always been at variance with the world. It was two thousand years ago, it was a hundred years ago, and it is today, probably in no greater degree than ever before. The problem is that we have been accommodating for two thousand years, and we have almost nothing left to give away. We are almost at the bare minimum of our faith.

This is why these words from Paul are important now more than ever:

> I appeal to you, therefore, brothers and sisters, by the mercies of God, to present your bodies as a living sacrifice, holy and acceptable to God, which is your spiritual worship. Do not be conformed to this world, but be transformed by the renewing of your minds, so that you might discern what is the will of God—what is good and acceptable and perfect. (Romans 12:1–2)

"Be not conformed to this world"! But we are!

Sunday after Sunday, we Christians give our witness to the world. We smile for the tourists, we maintain the outward show, our quaint traditions now divorced by many centuries from their origins. Young folks leave us. Sometimes we do a good business, but a lot of what we have to offer is cheese.

And our churches, I suppose, are museums.

—∞—

What does it mean for you to be a Christian? It meant a great deal to Jacob Amman, the Mennonite bishop who inspired the Amish movement. A modest man himself, he insisted on absolute plainness of dress, considering buttons an affectation; that's why originally the Amish were known as *Häftler* (hook-and-eyers) and their cousins the Mennonites as *Knöfler* (button people). Further differences led to the forming of sects: the Old Order Amish and the Old Order Mennonites, the Beachy Amish Mennonites, and the Hutterites, among many others.

But although their sect began in opposition, the Amish seek modesty and gentleness. They do not accept higher education, fearing that it leads to pride. They drive buggies rather than automobiles for the simplicity and closeness to Creation. They are "in the world, but not of it," living as "strangers" and "pilgrims," deliberately making a witness. Everything about them—their dress, their language, their work, their worship—speaks to what they will pass on to their children. At some point their traditions must seem absurd to us—who cares if clothes have buttons?—but these traditions are merely metaphors for the cause of Christ. The Amish believe that they have a twofold responsibility: to be different from the world, and to pass those differences on. For them, that is an important part of what it means to be a Christian.

Amish children are actually given quite wide latitude so that when they come of age they may freely choose whether to remain in this way of life or to take up the culture around them. This is what some of them have said:

> "I didn't fit in with the Amish young people and I sort of despised them for their lack of learning."
>
> "I wanted to go to high school so badly I remember crying about it. I knew I would never stay Amish—I wanted to be more than a farmer."
>
> "Tourists come in here and think we are angels or better than other people, and expect to see us floating several feet off the ground."
>
> "I just don't enjoy living in a museum or zoo, whatever you would call it."[11]

I suppose Christian kids anywhere are torn between a desire to be different and a need to be the same. If we want them to "be not conformed to this world," then we had better have a clear understanding of their "living sacrifice" and what it means to be a Christian.

—⟋ฑ—

That means we must decide which values are essential. While we Methodists didn't get too exercised about buttons or buggies, we used to have prohibitions against dancing and card-playing. Were those values essential? No, and the world didn't think so, either. Our witness for such things came to nothing.

But the essential values of the Amish have attracted and kept Amish children against great odds. It's amazing that many of them still choose to live modestly and meaningfully. They choose not to make great wealth their life's pursuit. They dedicate themselves to nonviolence, to family, and community; indeed, every aspect of their lives is a faithful witness.

These should be broadly shared human values. But because they are not, they must be at least broadly shared Christian values, or we do not deserve the name of Christ.

If we hope to keep our kids as Christians, I can think of no better way than for us to live recognizably as Christians. We all have seen enough of worldly churchgoers indistinguishable from those who profess no faith at all. Methodists, Baptists, Catholics, whoever we are, we may find that the difficulty of our faith is part of its appeal. The essential life has always been attractive.

Young people might not be interested in beards and buttons and buggies, but it seems to me that most—not all, but most—want to be transformed by the renewing of their minds, so that they might discern what is the will of God, what is good and acceptable and perfect. Anything less would be too easy, or even cheesy—as any kid will tell you.

Jesus and Mrs. Fish

*M*rs. Stuyvesant Fish of Fifth Avenue, New York, and Newport, Rhode Island, did not usually drive her own automobile. However, she was determined to learn, and all her house staff stood by as she tried. No sooner had she started the engine than she ran over a servant. Flustered, she threw the car into reverse, felt a thud as she ran over him again, and as the poor man staggered to his feet, she changed gears and ran over him a third time.

At the turn of the twentieth century there was no income tax, and the very rich—the Astors and Vanderbilts and Morgans—entered upon a Gilded Age. Fur traders and meat packers and chewing gum kings lived like aristocrats. At a time when the average American family earned $340 a year, the William K. Vanderbilts built a summer home at Newport which took four years to create at a cost of $11 million. The home employed butlers, chefs, maids, valets, footmen, stableboys, coachmen, grooms, nannies, governesses, social secretaries, gardeners, and yacht crews.

Mr. Ward McAllister, the ultimate arbiter for the nouveau riche, said, "There are really only four hundred people in New York society," and made it his life's work to maintain an actual list. Among the Four Hundred were Mrs. William Backhouse Astor Jr., always referred to as *The* Mrs. Astor, and the triumvirate of Newport society: Mrs. Hermann Oelrichs, Mrs. O.H.P. Belmont, and Mrs. Stuyvesant Fish. With each summer's entertainments, they tried to outdo one another. At one home, the center of the table was covered with sand; at each place was a small sterling silver pail with matching shovel. At a given signal half a hundred guests dug frantically into the sand in front of them for their favors—thousands of dollars' worth of rubies, sapphires, emeralds and diamonds.[12]

To celebrate the Astor Cup in 1904, Mrs. Hermann Oelrichs hosted a White Ball. The Oelrichs' cottage, Rosecliff, was decorated all in white; all the guests came dressed in white. Mrs. Oelrichs had asked the U.S. Navy to anchor its "White Fleet" just offshore from

her seafront home, but when it had declined, she had hired carpenters to build a dozen full-size ships, for this night only, simply to provide a fine backdrop with their full white sails.

Mrs. Stuyvesant Fish of Newport, Rhode Island, like other society hostesses, budgeted (if that is the word) upwards of $200,000 a season for entertaining. That was the money then. Today, of course, it would be worth ten times that. But Mamie, as she was known, professed herself unimpressed with money, impatient with high society, bored with ostentation. Her husband, president of the Illinois Central Railroad, still had to work for a living. "We're not really rich," she said. "We have only a few million." While everyone else in her social circle knew everyone well, she pretended not to remember their names.

> She would always welcome guests to her balls with an impatient "Howdy do, howdy do," moving them along with obvious annoyance. "Make yourselves at home," she said, "and believe me, there is no one who wishes you were there more than I do."[13]

Thumbing her nose at Newport's leisurely pace, Mrs. Fish regularly served eight-course meals in less than an hour; once she had guests bolt down dinner in thirty minutes.

But for all her refreshing simplicity, Mrs. Fish could also entertain with bewildering extravagance. She claimed to have little use for society; at the same time, she wanted to overwhelm it. She saw its values as trivial and senseless, but then she could throw a lavish party for her friends' dogs and provide her own dog with a $15,000 diamond collar. And with little concern for the feelings of her house staff, she hosted a Servants' Ball in which society folks dressed as doormen, coachmen, and scullery maids.

So she had mixed feelings about money. I don't know that she had a very profound spiritual life, but Jesus came for Mrs. Stuyvesant Fish.

—◊◊◊—

It's no coincidence that Jesus' message appealed to prosperous people. They had not found satisfaction or meaning in their own lives, and were moved by his simple life. Jesus represented a kind of novelty, which is always in demand.

One day a well-off man asked him, "What must I do to be saved?" Jesus gave him the obvious answer, known to all Jews: the Ten Commandments. Proudly, the man said he had kept them all. Then Jesus tested the man with a drastic suggestion that forced him to face what really was the god in his life.

> A certain ruler asked him, "Good Teacher, what must I do to inherit eternal life?" Jesus said to him, "Why do you call me good? No one is good but God alone. You know the commandments: 'You shall not commit adultery; You shall not murder; You shall not steal; You shall not bear false witness; Honor your father and mother.'" He replied, "I have kept all these since my youth." When Jesus heard this, he said to him, "There is still one thing lacking. Sell all that you own and distribute the money to the poor, and you will have treasure in heaven; then come, follow me." But when the man heard this, he became sad; for he was very rich. Jesus looked at him and said, "How hard it is for those who have wealth to enter the kingdom of God! Indeed, it is easier for a camel to go through the eye of a needle than for someone who is rich to enter the kingdom of God."
>
> Those who heard it said, "Then who can be saved?" He replied, "What is impossible for mortals is possible for God." (Luke 18:18–27)

This is one of Jesus' very hardest sayings. It was so hard that even his disciples were not sure about it.

We are all like Mrs. Fish. We pretend to despise ostentation, and we say that money doesn't matter, but we also crave these things. We listen to Jesus' teachings about money, knowing full well that we will never apply them. Sell all we have and give the money to the poor? Many Christians are offended at the suggestion. We want to know why. Why does Jesus ask this?

Well, I suppose it's possible that he meant to redistribute wealth. After all, as we read in the Book of Acts, the early Christians did sell all their goods and distribute the proceeds to those who had need. In modern America, it's a possibility we don't much like to consider, but I think an honest reading of the Bible requires it.

It is also possible that Jesus proposed a religious discipline, not unlike the fasting he had done in the desert and which we continue every Lent. In every age some Christians have taken vows of poverty.

But I think Jesus was up to something else. He had located our soft spot, the god of our lives, what we truly believe in. He knew the universal belief that money will save us, that it will make us important, that money will make our lives more pleasant, that there can never be too much of it. Of all the false gods in the world, this is the hardest to give up.

So must we give up our possessions to be saved? The disciples knew that no one would do that. They asked, "Who then can be saved?" The problem is not just for the rich, but for all of us, the middle-class and poor as well.

Listen closely: Jesus said, "What is impossible for human beings is possible for God."

Truly, we will not be saved by giving up anything. We will never be saved by what we do, however good or selfless. Jesus had suggested this only to point out our false gods, our misplaced faith. No, we are saved by the cross. It pays the price. And it reorders our priorities—if we believe in it.

I think this is incredible—but Jesus died for Mrs. Stuyvesant Fish. She did not carry his cross—it cost her nothing. It costs you just what it cost her—everything, if you truly believe in it.

—⁓—

A little while back we enjoyed some rich times. Not every last person prospered, but very many did. Middle-class folks who had lived alongside wealth and ostentation finally got a piece of it. Even today, many folks are better off than ever before. Up where I live, or rather, just around the bay, the boom times are building a modern Newport.

Maybe you are wondering, What should I do with my wealth?

Well, of course I could suggest some worthy outlets. The tithe, made to all kinds of charities, is still very important. But I don't think that's all that Jesus had in mind.

What should you do with your nest egg? Forsake it; give it up; if not in deed, then in heart; forsake what cannot save you. That nest egg cannot save your soul, nor give you complete peace or purpose. If you cannot forsake it, then just *forget* about it for a moment, and ask a different question, for this concern over mere money means that you haven't found your true wealth.

This is what Jesus was getting at. We must discover our true wealth, and ask the really important question: *What should I do with the cross?*

When we ask it that way, our lives look very different indeed.

—〜〜—

Those who measure themselves by the size of their houses are a long ways from the wealth of the cross.

Mrs. William K. Vanderbilt once declared, "I know of no profession, art or trade that women are working in today as taxing on one's mental resources as being a leader of society." But her parties didn't always turn out as planned. At one costume ball, a smallish man arrived, dressed as Henry the IV, with his rotund wife dressed as a Norman peasant. The confused footman announced: *"Henry IV and an enormous pheasant."*

Nor did it always work out for Mrs. Stuyvesant Fish. On the morning after one of her parties, the society page of the *New York Herald* accidentally switched her guest list for a list of people who had attended a prize fight at Madison Square Garden. Mob figures in her ballroom, with the Drexels and Vanderbilts at ringside!

Maybe it served her right, for while half the country struggled to put a decent meal on the table, she was spending great sums so that a baby elephant in her dining room could reach for the bowl of nuts. Even high society wasn't sure what to do when Mrs. Fish sat a doll at every other place at the table, and limited the conversation at her soiree to baby talk. Obviously she wanted to be saved—from boredom, from the confines of polite society—so her efforts were a little desperate.

Really, in the eyes of God, the things we do with our money may seem little less bizarre. Very often we are uncertain of what to do with it. We middle-class folks especially should have discovered a long time ago wealth beyond displays of wealth, beyond our small nest eggs. You and I may not think ourselves rich, but we know that Jesus is speaking to us when he asks us to give up that old false god. We have a greater treasure.

It is an ordinary plank of wood, about as long as your arms.

I think this is incredible—Jesus died for us. You and I did not carry his cross—it cost us nothing. And yet it costs us everything, if we take it as our own.

Cross at the Light

*T*he last words spoken by film actor Douglas Fairbanks were, "I've never felt better." Civil War General John Sedgwick said, "They couldn't hit an elephant at this dist—" Dylan Thomas, bragged just before he collapsed, "I've had eighteen straight whiskies. I think that's the record." And as he lay dying in a shabby hotel room, Oscar Wilde declared, "Either that wallpaper goes, or I do."

Most of us don't choose the last right words, but occasionally some of us do say something instructive. President William McKinley's wife knelt at his bedside and sobbed, "I want to go too, I want to go too." McKinley told her, "We are all going." And when Grace Kelly bent to kiss her dying uncle, he whispered softly, "My dear, before you kiss me . . . fix your hair. It's a mess."

The best last words I know of come from a short story by Judy Troy. A family has gathered to say goodbye to the grandfather, and a young girl, who has lost her father, is talking with her Aunt Mavis Jean:

> "Come help me get some coffee and cake," Mavis Jean said to me.
> I followed her into the kitchen, and when she picked up the coffeepot I saw that her hands were shaking.
> "I can do that," I said.
> She went over to the sloping counter under the window, looking off into the dark back yard. Then she turned around and looked at me.

"What was it like," she asked softly, "having your daddy die?"
" 'Cross at the light, Roberta,' " I said. "That was the last thing he said to me."
"That has some sweetness in it," she said. "Sweetness and good advice."[14]

—⚏—

All over town we've seen them—crossing guards in orange vests, blowing whistles and raising stop signs so that a few small children can cross two lanes to safety. The children look left and see traffic going one way. They look right and see traffic going another. When the street is clear, the children cross—and with this good example, they cross other streets on their way home.

Some kids don't notice where they're going. They would run into a cement mixer if it weren't for the crossing guard. Others may be more careful, may even help the crossing guard to look, until something distracts them.

And then they're gone. A few words on both sides: "Bye." "See you." "Thanks." The crossing guard is the last adult at school to speak to them that day. Most of us don't choose our words that carefully, but that adult wants to say something instructive, something with sweetness and good advice.

—⚏—

Everything Jesus said had the force of last words. From the gospel records it appears that nothing he said was wasted. We get the sense that he was always conscious of the infinite worth of each listener and the brief moment he had with them.

In our scripture today, Jesus is asked, "Who is the greatest in the kingdom of heaven?" This is not the kind of question asked by a spiritually serious individual. It is instead an idle, selfish question.

But Jesus does not dismiss the questioner as easily as I have just done. Jesus sees the questioner as a person of infinite worth, and offers some good advice:

At that time the disciples came to Jesus and asked, "Who is the greatest in the kingdom of heaven?" He called a child, whom he put among them, and said, "Truly, I tell you, unless you change and become like children, you will never enter the kingdom of heaven. Whoever becomes humble like this child is the greatest in the kingdom of heaven. Whoever welcomes one such child in my name welcomes me." (Matthew 18:1–5)

When we become like children, we realize how much we depend on God and how much others depend on us. The kingdom of God is built by how we support and instruct one another. This is why Jesus immediately follows his good advice with a word of warning. If you let a child go the wrong way, you do it at great peril:

"If any of you put a stumbling block before one of these little ones who believe in me, it would be better for you if a great millstone were fastened around your neck and you were drowned in the depth of the sea. Woe to the world because of stumbling blocks! Occasions for stumbling are bound to come, but woe to the one by whom the stumbling comes!" (Matthew 18:6–7)

Now, most of us believe that Jesus is talking about someone else. We think that, in modern terms, the stumbling blocks for our kids must be drugs and gangs and sex. But really Jesus is speaking to us. We are the stumbling blocks, and our fault is silence.

We make sure that children cross the street safely. But how do we care for their spiritual safety? This world can be so confusing and dangerous for them. The traffic whizzes one way, the traffic whizzes another way—a child could get hurt or worse.

We should be giving them some sweetness and good advice, and helping them to cross at the light. Yet we are often afraid to tell them about the things that really matter. Afraid of bringing up our faith because we don't want to impose it on them. Afraid that we lost our chance some time ago. Afraid of their disrespect.

So we limit ourselves to a few words as they go speeding on their way—words of one syllable: "Bye." "See you." "Thanks."

—m—

Now, I don't want to be morbid, but have you thought about your last words? Well, you're right; you might not get to choose them.

So instead, what would be your *first* words? If you had the opportunity to tell a young person something important today, what's the first thing you would say? What would be your words to live by?

Maybe you'd say, "Whites in hot water, colors in cold." Maybe you'd say, "The secret of wealth is compound interest." "Keep your knees together on your first date." "It's as easy to marry a rich girl as a poor one." "Measure twice, cut once."

The novelist John Updike says that some of the best advice he ever got from his father came one day while they were making sandwiches. His father, who had worked his way through college in a cafeteria, told him, "Butter toward the edges. Enough gets in the middle anyway."

Those are indeed good words to live by, and they certainly would stand a novelist in good stead. However, maybe you're not in the habit of handing out such homely words. That will work to your benefit and give special force to the moment when you tell a child about your faith. It only takes one time, if the time is right. A friend of mine never hid from his family his relationship with God, although he rarely said much about it. One day his teenage daughter was telling him that she had decided to drop a class in which she wasn't doing too well.

At last he said: "You might want to get a second opinion."

The girl gave him a sour look. "What do you mean? I know what I'm doing."

"Well, that may be, but you might want to get a second opinion."

"Dad—I'm not going to some doctor."

"Just think about what I said."

"You mean ask the teacher what he thinks?"

"Possibly."

"You mean ask a friend? Or you or Mom?"

"That too, maybe."

"You mean . . ." And here she stopped.

"I mean," he said, "that when I wake up in the morning and when I go to bed at night, I ask for a second opinion."

And her eyes registered his words.

It's your job as a parent to tell children about your faith, in whatever words are right for you. The other side of this exchange is trust. You can't always be there. You *shouldn't* always be there. But it's good to know that they will always have someone else to offer sweetness and good advice.

Just a word—sometimes that's all we have. Just a word before the bus comes or the friends come or a lifetime comes and then they're gone, out the door and on their way.

Lost and Found

*M*y wife's brother Bill was no saint. He would tell a dirty joke to his grandmother, and tell it so she would laugh. He had scheme after scheme for fixing up cars, one lemon after another. He didn't wear underwear, either.

The first time we met, I was picking Rexene up for a date, and this big guy with a goatee opened the front door, holding a cup from the 7-Eleven. Bill was a bouncer at a bar, and right then he looked like the bouncer at his own house. From his height he inspected me, took a sip, and said, "You don't look that cute." And then he gave me his smile, which, I have to admit, might have affected different people in different ways, but put me at ease.

He was an independent, irreverent kind of guy, and never seemed to lack for a place to go or friends to see. His sisters were a little awed, I think, by his social life. And even though his friends and family were very loyal to him, it's safe to say that he had made mistakes and done some things for which they hadn't yet forgiven him.

Just after All Saints' Day, Bill was killed as the passenger in an auto accident. He left behind all those unfinished relationships.

I remember his Uncle Bill, the big funny man for whom he was named, weeping as he thought about how just a few days before they had celebrated their birthdays together. There was even leftover birthday cake around the house, and it tasted pretty bitter.

The woman who would become my wife also wept for many sleepless days, overcome with what she had lost.

—⚬⚬—

Nothing in God's creation is ever lost. This is a physical fact. Matter is turned to energy; energy is imparted to matter. Some people take comfort in realizing that in the physical world, nothing is ever lost to God.

But for others of us, it may be small comfort to think that God knows where our loved ones have gone; as far as we are concerned, they are lost to us. We want to find them again. And we look everywhere. We look in our own grief. We may be terribly fatigued by grief, but we don't dare let go of it, for fear of losing the person all over again. We return to the past, we search the past, we scour the past.

The psalmist says, "I will seek God in the land of the living." That may also be the best place to find people we have loved, because their lives have not been theirs alone. Paul wrote to the Romans:

> None of us lives to himself, and none of us dies to himself. If we live, we live to the Lord, and if we die, we die to the Lord; so then, whether we live or whether we die, we are the Lord's. For to this end Christ died and lived again, that he might be Lord both of the dead and of the living. (Romans 14:7–9 RSV)

Paul, an imperfect man who became known as *Saint* Paul, was writing about loved ones who reveal God in the world, whether or not they are aware of doing so.

All those unfinished relationships are not lost forever. The gospel is that they can be found.

As Christians we honor certain people who have shaped our lives, whose love and presence are with us still, and we call them saints—not because they were perfect, but because their lives were not wasted on us. I can think of no better evidence of God's existence than the fact that lives are not wasted. In a world without

God, lives would be cheap and quickly forgotten, but they are not.
They certainly are not.

—ᴍ—

Jesus died one thousand, nine hundred and some years ago. Some
of us may feel that Jesus lived and died so long ago that he is lost
to us—that we can never really know him. After all, he belonged
to a vanished world of dusty towns filled with sheep, beggars, lep-
ers, soldiers, and nomadic merchants. . . .

Yet Jesus is woven into our lives today, into the very fabric of
the present moment. It's remarkable—if you really prepare yourself for Communion, you join Jesus at the table as he breaks the
bread and pours the cup and speaks the Passover blessing, and then
says something extraordinary: "This is my body . . . this is my
blood." Jesus becomes real to you as a friend, and the Lord's Supper becomes inexpressibly poignant.

Taste the bread. It is not so different from what the apostles
tasted. Taste the wine. It hasn't changed much over the centuries.
We are not so different from the men and women who knew Jesus,
who brought to him their complex natures and mixed motives.
Like them, we are ordinary people, and like them we are called to
be saints.

—ᴍ—

Saints are not perfect people; actually, I'm not sure what a perfect
person would be. All saints are sinners. We do recognize a few
great men and women who have been associated with miracles, but
really when we call people saints we honor the extraordinary
nature of ordinary people.

They change our lives. In modest ways they remind us that the
world is a good place—that love has a transforming power—and
so make it easier for us to believe in God. These wonderful, imperfect people leave deep marks on us, and we grieve them until grief

leaves its mark, too. Sometimes we have to forgive them for leaving abruptly or for leaving things undone.

Once as I was getting acquainted with a parish, I called on a woman who lived alone in a place too big for her. Fresh flowers stood on a table and Hummel figurines on shelves, but other items— such as a gun case—didn't jibe with the rest. She explained to me that her husband had dropped dead at home.

"That idiot," she said, unconvincingly, "left me with a side of beef in the freezer."

"When was that?" I asked innocently.

"Six years ago," she said. "Now my kids are grown and gone, and all my recipes are for six. There's brisket and flank steak, filets, stew meat, porterhouse steaks, and about forty pounds of ground beef in there. I can't bring myself to eat it and can't give it away, either. It was his idea to get this stuff. 'We'll go through it in no time,' he said. He's probably laughing like he always did whenever he stuck me with one of his crazy schemes. The next time I see him, he's getting some freezer-burned pot roast."

Talk about unfinished relationships—just consider how the disciples felt about Jesus. Imagine their bewilderment and anger at a man who had thrown away everything, including them, for a suicidal march into Jerusalem. It seems that Jesus anticipated their feelings, and reassured them, "You shall not be comfortless." He described the Passover bread and wine as his own body and blood, and added, "As often as you take this, do so in remembrance of me." (As often as you take the Passover meal? As often as you take any bread or wine?)

They saw him after his death, and found his presence everywhere: in the bread, in the wine, in other faces. In fact, I believe our relationship with him will never be finished.

—ɯ—

Rexene often marks All Saints' Sunday with her family. I talked with her by phone last night. She passed along some terrible jokes from them. (Bill would've been proud.) And the family celebrated

Uncle Bill's birthday. I imagine that they had a cake, and that it tasted pretty good.

Of course they are thinking about someone who isn't there. His laughter is probably shaping the conversation even now, all these years later.

A saint? Oh, for God's sake, we knew him too well to call him a *saint*. And yet, if sainthood is measured by such love, then maybe we have known a few.

The next time you prepare to take the Lord's meal, rediscover someone who has seemed far away. It might be someone in your family, or a friend who died years ago. It might be Jesus.

Cherish the communion of the saints . . . the communion of the saints . . . the communion of the saints . . .

> . . . the forgiveness of sins . . .
> . . . the resurrection of the body . . .
> . . . and the life everlasting. Amen.

A Light in the House

*T*his is a love story about Elizabeth Whitney Williams, the first lighthouse keeper up where I live. It's about a pioneer girl's love for her parents, her siblings, and her two husbands. She was born on Mackinac Island in 1844. One of her earliest memories was of being rowed from Mackinac to the mainland of the Upper Peninsula—a long way to row, especially in November:

> One cold, still morning in November our boat was prepared and we started to Manistique. Charley and I were again placed in among warm blankets. . . . The day was cold and still. Father and the boys rowed while Mother steered. We kept close to the shore. I can hear my father even now singing his old hymns, "Rock of Ages" and "The Evergreen Shore." Mother, too, sang her French glee songs. . . .
>
> As we neared the shore, men stood ready to meet us. . . . Our house was all warmed up with a nice fire going in the great stone fireplace. Lights were lighted and supper was soon ready for us all, beds were put up, and soon we felt we were at home.[15]

It seems the family often had perilous trips over the Great Lakes, and even on land. When news came that a friend had died, Mr. and Mrs. Whitney insisted on paying their respects, even though it meant a fifteen-mile walk in a blinding blizzard. They trudged along the icy lakeshore as night set in. Wolves howled in the distance. Mrs. Whitney grew faint. Their only hope was a fishing shanty a mile and a half further on, and even that might no longer be there. Mr. Whitney threw down his pack, his saw, and gun, and carried his wife through the knee-deep snow with wolves drawing closer. At the very last moment before they were over-taken, they found the shanty. Wolves howled all around and scratched the door.

Mr. Whitney found a flint and a tin lamp full of fish oil, and there in the very depths of the wilderness they held each other and made it through the night till they set out at morning to care for their grieving friends.

As I said, this is a love story. Late in her life, Libby Whitney Williams wrote this down, mindful of how it and similar events shaped her career as the keeper of a lighthouse.

Our pioneer ancestors who settled this territory when it was rough, rude, dangerous, and naked to the elements—our pioneer fathers and mothers knew the value of home. A light in the home told them that God was near. And to those who sailed the inland seas, who tempted the Great Lakes with their small craft, a light-house signaled that love was near.

Perhaps we take the light in a home for granted; perhaps we take the home itself for granted until we too are shut out in the elements, and then we find how important it is to keep the lovelight burning. Libby Williams knew; and so did some of our other ancestors in the faith.

—◆—

Which brings us to the letter to the Hebrews. The title of this let-ter, in itself, is curious. For hundreds of years the people of Israel had called themselves Jews. Long ago they had been Hebrews, and had escaped from Egypt with Moses, then wandered in the wilder-ness for forty years as the pioneers of a promised land. As they had become settled and prosperous, their character and mission had changed, and they had become Jews.

Now their promised land was torn by war; Jerusalem lay in ruins; the Temple had been destroyed; the people of Israel had been scattered throughout the Roman Empire in a dispersion called the

Diaspora, and cast out into the wilderness of a hostile world where they would wander until the reestablishment of Israel in 1947. As they wandered, they wondered why God would make them pilgrims again.

So the author comforted them. Like the Hebrews, they would have hard lives, yet their struggles would be part of God's plan, the beginning of something great. The letter recounted all Hebrew history and its culmination in Christ:

> It was fitting that God, for whom and through whom all things exist, in bringing many children to glory, should make the pioneer of their salvation perfect through sufferings. For the one who sanctifies and those who are sanctified have one Father. For this reason Jesus is not ashamed to call them brothers and sisters, saying, "I will proclaim your name to my brothers and sisters, in the midst of the congregation I will praise you." And again, "I will put my trust in him." And again, "Here am I and the children whom God has given me." (Hebrews 2:10–13)

Early Christians saw themselves as pioneers, with the civilizing force of love. They were what their Hebrew ancestors had been—in the words of Isaiah, "a light to the nations."

—ᴍ—

Libby Whitney beat the odds. She survived her childhood, and as a young woman found a suitable man in the lighthouse keeper at Beaver Island.

> Our tower was built round with a winding stair of iron steps. My husband having now very poor health I took charge of the care of the lamps, and the beautiful lens in the tower was my especial care. On stormy nights I watched the light that no accident might happen. We burned the lard oil, which needed great care, especially in cold weather, when the oil would congeal and fail to flow fast enough to the wicks. In long nights the lamps had to be trimmed twice, and sometimes oftener. At such times the light needed careful watching. From the first the work always had a fascination for me. I loved the water, having always been

near it, and I loved to stand in the tower and watch the great rolling waves chasing and tumbling in upon the shore.[16]

He was drowned trying to rescue a crew of fishermen. Libby, his young widow, was asked to take over for him.

Fortunately she found another love, and in September 1875, she married Dan Williams. He was her great friend, her life companion; he gladly cared for her mother, who lived to the age of one hundred. In the unlikeliest of places, they shared civilization, for they both made music: he played the fiddle, she the piano. In the unlikeliest of houses, they made a home, and they never took it for granted.

They remained at Beaver Island until 1884. That year she was placed in charge of the new Harbor Point lighthouse, just a little walk from where I live.

—∽—

Truly the wilderness is not conquered with axe or plow. It is overcome by love. No place—no matter how remote, no matter the latitude—no place need be without love.

Our ancestors wandered in the wilderness of a loveless world and overcame it with their love. Why would we allow that to be extinguished?

Lately we have wandered again in a loveless world; we have returned to the wilderness. In an almost literal sense for many people, the wolves are at the door; their dangers are very real.

I deal now with young single mothers who scrape together rent money from food money, who balance jobs against day care, who have a hard time dating again without giving their kids false hopes or bad lessons. I deal with young men who have never seen a man treat a woman with respect and instead try on a variety of poses. These people don't know how to love, and it tears them apart.

Their ancestors fought for them to have the homes that they now wreck so casually. Their great-grandparents tried so hard to escape the violence they invite so readily.

Our role as a church is to help them find a way through these problems; to make a path, build a home, and make it safe; and to find their help in a community. Who knows what sort of a world they will live in tomorrow? What comforts, what dangers, what possibilities will they encounter? The human heart is the same in every age and is ever in need of civilizing. Like the early Christians who found themselves in the role of their Hebrew ancestors, we must clear a way in the modern wilderness.

Libby kept the Harbor Point lighthouse until 1906, having spent forty-four years in the lighthouse service. She had seen the area go from a desolate wilderness to an affluent resort. Thanks to pioneers like Dan and herself who had provided a safe harbor, a town had grown up around them and lights shone in a hundred homes around the bay.

In her later years she was Michigan's oldest resident, but the sparkle in her eyes made her seem younger.

As I say, this is a love story. Although they both had been married before, they were married sixty-two years. *Sixty-two years.*

When Dan died in 1937, it took Libby only twenty-four hours to join him. It was an age of honking horns and platinum blondes and swinging jazz, but it still had some of the civilizing force of love.

The lighthouse is no longer tended. I serve a church within sight of it. The bell tower and the beacon speak to each other about the pioneer days, which are now.

Winter

A True Likeness

*T*here's a charming story about the Buddha, a truly humble man who insisted that his followers make no image or portrait of him. One day a young follower found him on the banks of the Ganges River, deep in contemplation. The Buddha's pose was so serene and profound that the young man longed to paint him. He reasoned that if he painted not the Buddha, but the Buddha's *reflection in the water*, that would be all right. So to this day many pictures of the Buddha are rippled, as if they were reflections.

It's a shame that no one two thousand years ago painted an authentic likeness of Jesus. The English historian Thomas Carlyle once wrote:

> Though I am a poor man, I would gladly give a third of what I have for an accurate representation of Jesus' physical appearance. Had these carvers of marble chiseled a faithful statue of the Son of Man . . . and shown us what manner of man he was like, what his height, what his build and what the features of his face were, I would have thanked the sculptor with all the gratitude of my heart for that portrait as the most precious heirloom of the ages.[17]

That powerful wish is what gave rise to the legend of Veronica, a woman of Jerusalem who wept for Jesus as he carried the cross through the city streets. According to the legend, she gave him a handkerchief to wipe his bloody brow, and when he handed it back, it was stained with the likeness of his face. Thereafter she was called Veronica, *vera icon* meaning "true likeness."

Surely you know the legend of the Shroud of Turin, an ancient burial cloth that has been stained with the photographic negative of a crucified man, such as might have been produced in a burst of energy at
the resurrection. For hundreds of years, many people believed that it
was the burial cloth of Jesus, that it showed what Jesus looked like.
The Vatican allowed the Shroud to be tested by modern methods and
learned that it probably dates to the middle ages.

It has been hard for us to find the true likeness of Christ. In early
Christian art, Jesus looked severe and not too young—he had an
angry, challenging stare. In medieval art, he was very young and
benign, even wan. In the art of the high Renaissance, with painters
such as Michelangelo, Jesus was a powerfully built, virile man,
while in Victorian art he was a baby. The way that Jesus is represented depends on the fashion of the day.

In 1892, a French painter named Leon Lhermitte painted a
portrait of Jesus that showed him in biblical garb but seated at a
table with French peasants in the year 1892. These Frenchmen
crowded around the table, marveling at their strange visitor, the
historical Jesus. This picture became popular here in the United
States when it was reproduced in *Ladies' Home Journal* in
December 1922. There it was seen by an American artist named
Warner Sallman. He was so taken with it that he made his own
reproduction in charcoal. Years later, in 1940 Sallman did his
own portrait of Christ, using his charcoal study and the original
painting by Lhermitte.

He took out the French peasants, took out the table, took out
Christ's long robe, and everything else, had Christ lower his gaze
and look off to one side. The final portrait showed only Jesus'
shoulders and head. In fact, Sallman called his portrait *Head of
Christ.*

Many people think of this as Jesus' official portrait.

Why do they find it so authentic? Maybe because it resembles
other official portraits. In fact, it looks like something done by
Olan Mills. Consider the studio lighting, the fair complexion and
rosy lips, his blue eyes. This is not a very Jewish Jesus. And yet
Warner Sallman's picture of Jesus has been distributed almost one
billion times. Of all the masterpieces of Christian art, it's an

unlikely favorite, yet so many people say, "That must be what Jesus looked like."

—〰—

It's hard to get a likeness of Jesus from the gospels. They present four views of him, all different in some way. He is elusive, he turns and is gone; the stories seem sketched of shadows, movement, overheard conversations. Jesus is at once close, yet distant.

And that's not only the experience of readers today. It seems from the stories that this is how his contemporaries experienced him, too. Throughout the gospels, people ask, "Who is this man? Who is he?"

Consider the experience of Pontius Pilate. He was roused early one morning (and it's safe to assume that Pilate was not a morning man), obliged to deal with a complaint brought by Jewish leaders he didn't much admire. He himself cared little for religious affairs. But he did manage to summon enough wits to ask a few perfunctory questions and to put Jesus through a faintly boring interrogation:

> Then Pilate entered the headquarters again, summoned Jesus, and asked him, "Are you the King of the Jews?" Jesus answered, "Do you ask this on your own, or did others tell you about me?" Pilate answered, "I am not a Jew, am I? Your own nation and the chief priests have handed you over to me. What have you done?" Jesus answered, "My kingdom is not [of] this world. If my kingdom were [of] this world, my followers would be fighting to keep me from being handed over to the Jews. But as it is, my kingdom is not [of] here." Pilate asked him, "So you are a king?" Jesus answered, "You say that I am a king. For this I was born, and for this I came into the world, to testify to the truth. Everyone who belongs to the truth listens to my voice." Pilate asked him, "What is truth?" (John 18:33–38)

If ever a question didn't stay for an answer, it was this question. Pilate asked idly, rhetorically, "What is truth?" and then walked away, the question still ringing in the air.

It seemed that Pilate had the last, cynical word—but he didn't. For Jesus had turned the question around. Pilate had asked him, "Are you the King of the Jews?" Jesus had answered him, *I am about the truth. I came to testify to the truth. Whoever listens to my voice hears the truth.*

Perhaps it wasn't going to do any good to remove his face from the crowd.

—⁓—

In their provinces, the Romans tried to separate church and state. You could be a Jew, but not King of the Jews—not unless you were Caesar. You could pay homage to your God as long as you paid taxes to Caesar—and Caesar's likeness was on each coin. Remember how some Jews asked Jesus if they should pay taxes, and he showed them a Roman coin and asked, "Whose image is this?" And everyone could say, "Oh, that's Caesar, of course." Caesar was instantly recognizable.

No one could say that about Jesus. Some thought he was Elijah or one of the prophets; some said he was a devil. Both before and after his resurrection even some of his followers could not recognize him. Thomas insisted that Jesus prove himself by showing his wounds; only then would he believe that this likeness, this apparition before him, was truly the Christ. As we read in the Gospel of John, Jesus convinced him, but not before reminding him that the truth is larger than what we see and touch.

> He said to Thomas, "Put your finger here and see my hands. Reach out your hand and put it in my side. Do not doubt, but believe." Thomas answered him, "My Lord and my God!" Jesus said to him, "Have you believed because you have seen me? Blessed are those who have not seen and yet have come to believe." (John 20:27–29, au. trans.)

—⁓—

A few years ago, a high school student named Eric Pensinger was troubled to find Sallman's *Head of Christ* hanging in the hallway of his high school in Bloomingdale, Michigan. It had been donated some thirty years before, a pretty inexpensive print, and it had always been displayed in an inexpensive but prominent frame in the most well traveled hallway in the school.

Well, the American Civil Liberties Union got involved, the school board got involved, and while this was a matter of legal dispute, the portrait was shrouded in velvet so folks couldn't see it—which only made it all the more conspicuous.

Until that time the community had never wondered whether a public school should display a portrait of Jesus. Pilate, of course, had a vested interest in separating church and state—but then so do churches today. What Eric Pensinger objected to was that Jesus' likeness in a school hallway was tantamount to an official portrait, like putting George Washington on the face of a coin. You have a sense that the person represented has some authority—and Eric Pensinger said, Not over me, he doesn't.

Should we see a portrait of Christ in a public school? I doubt that Eric Pensinger realized the religious profundity of his objection. It may never have occurred to him that Christians see the face of the risen Christ reflected in many people, that no single image has sole authority, that he cannot be limited to an image in a frame.

It's kind of ironic: at last the school board voted to settle out of court and to place beside Sallman's portrait similarly sized, similarly framed pictures of Abraham Lincoln and Martin Luther King Jr. So where there once had been one portrait of Jesus in Bloomingdale High School, now there are three.

—⟨⟨⟩⟩—

We have not seen the exact likeness of Christ, yet blessed are we who have not seen and yet believe! For even though it has not been given to us to see an accurate, literal representation of him, we have seen his reflection. Maybe there are ripples in that reflection.

Look around. Look among you, at people you love and who

have loved you back, who have shown you the truth and acted the truth. You don't have to go far to see him. We are created in the image of God and are called to be the body of Christ, and believe it or not, that is his true likeness.

One Light

*I*t gets dark early this time of year. In fact, I think that in northern Michigan sundown begins at two o'clock. The shadows lengthen, there's freezing at the doorstep, the lights never seem as bright as they did in the summer. Of course it is the season of death. Of course it is the wrong time for Christmas. But it is the birth of the Savior, just the same.

In this dark season, Christmas lights adorn our storefronts, our housefronts, our porches and trees. They represent, in a modest and modern way, something from a long time ago. Putting them up takes time, and if one light goes out, the whole string is shot. It's a delicate thing, but it proclaims the birth of the Savior, just the same.

It says that our lives are illumined. At Christmas long ago we received not many lights but one light, one mere, steady light that has lasted the centuries.

We can hardly imagine just how dark was the world into which the Savior was born. A tired tyrant sat on the rented throne of Judea, building his vanity with slave labor. The country leaked rebellion, and Rome tried to plug each leak with a legion of soldiers. If ever there was a season of death, that was one.

About this Savior, the prophet Isaiah had said, "The people who walked in darkness have seen a great light, and they who dwell in the land of the shadow of death, upon them has the light shined." And of him, the writer of the Fourth Gospel said, "The true light,

117

which enlightens everyone, was coming into the world." He also said, "The light shines in the darkness, and the darkness has not overcome it."

—◊—

Just a hundred and sixty years before the birth of Christ, it seemed that the Jewish faith would be extinguished. It was a season of death. For centuries the Jews had been persecuted, but never so terribly. The Syrian king Antiochus had invaded Jerusalem, plundered the city and burned it, seized the livestock, and taken women and children captive. Great numbers of Jewish men had been killed.

Antiochus now declared that all his many conquered kingdoms should be one people and surrender their customs. Jews would no longer be Jews. They would no longer practice their faith. Any who did not accept the new orders would be put to death. All the Gentiles accepted this command, and understandably many Jews did too.

Just to make sure, Antiochus sent his armies to every town and village to forbid circumcision and worship of the Hebrew God. In December of the year 167 BCE, they desecrated the Temple in Jerusalem and made sacrifices there to pagan gods.

Most Jews were content to surrender the Temple if it meant that they could live. Only a small band resisted, led by Mattathias and his five sons. They fought against great odds, and after their father died, Judas Maccabee and his brothers led the fight. And miraculously, they began to win. Though vastly outnumbered and fighting on the brink of starvation, his men won victory after victory until at last they retook Jerusalem.

Three years later, with the Temple rebuilt and the altar reconsecrated, the Jews gathered to give thanks. It was December of the year 164 BCE. Judas Maccabee called for eight days of celebration, beginning with the relighting of the Temple candles. But the Maccabees found just one small flask of oil, just enough to last one day at the most.

They burned the oil anyway. It burned through the first day . . .
and into the second . . .
and amazingly into the third . . .
and miraculously into the fourth . . .
into the fifth . . .
And they began to see the glory of God in their midst.

They had known such darkness. And now they saw a sign from God in just one light—one light that has lasted all these centuries. Without the faith and sacrifices of the Maccabees, it is possible that the Jewish faith might not have survived to the time of Jesus, let alone our own.

At sunset on the first night of Hanukkah, Jews all over the world light menorahs and begin the Festival of Lights. Like the lamp in the story, the Jewish people themselves persist and represent a miracle.

—⁓—

Faith is a kind of bravery. We can be threatened not just by a tyrant but by any kind of trouble—any illness, or job loss, or plan gone awry. What if we just gave up the fight? What if we never trusted God to provide resources after our own were gone?

The whole aim of faith is to brave trials with the strength of God. Other kinds of bravery come from confidence in ourselves, but the apostle Paul meant something very different when he said, "When I am weak, then I am strong." This is why we pray for God to deliver us from evil: to work a miracle.

Thirty-three years after his miraculous birth, Jesus entered Jerusalem, which had been defeated so many times. Although crowds cheered him, he was not caught up in the euphoria. He could foresee his death; perhaps he also foresaw the Jewish revolt of 69 CE which would fail, the Temple destroyed, the Jews scattered throughout the Roman Empire; it didn't require supernatural foresight to imagine such things. He urged people to make the most of his person and his presence:

> Jesus said to them, "The light is with you for a little longer. Walk while you have the light, so that the darkness may not overtake

you. If you walk in the darkness, you do not know where you
are going. While you have the light, believe in the light, so that
you may become children of light." (John 12:35–36)

Some of his listeners were going to lose everything except him.
The disciples certainly did, and still they were able to go on, in the
face of their own deaths, and tell a people waiting for hope that
Jesus was the one.

His disciples became "children of light" not by ordinary bravery, but by faith; not by representing themselves, but him; not on
their own power, but on his. There was only one of him, and that
was enough to work a miracle.

—ᶆ—

Christmas lights cast about as much light as a necklace of fireflies,
they tangle easily, and they're so fragile that all you have to do is
curse a little while putting them up and they decide not to work.
Fortunately, they come cheap—you can buy long strands of them
for $2.99—and electricity comes pretty cheap too, so you can keep
them blazing day and night.

Apparently we need more and more of these lights to hide the
dark heart where there used to be a holy day. A conspiracy of false
cheer often passes for Christmas—a banishment of worry, a denial
of trouble. It helps to sell merchandise, but this isn't very brave and
it isn't real faith.

While Christmas has grown more commercial, Hanukkah has
grown more significant and religious. The miracle of the Maccabees' lamp is very immediate for many Jews, who remember all
too well a season of death. Six million Jews perished in the Holocaust; many millions more perished in Stalin's pogroms. What
Antiochus began was almost accomplished. Nearly all the Jews of
Poland were killed, along with most of the Jews of the Ukraine,
Latvia, Lithuania, Hungary, Yugoslavia, Slovakia, Greece, the
Netherlands, and large numbers in France, Belgium, Russia, Ger-
many, and Austria.

Today there are only about thirteen million Jews in the world, less than the population of Madagascar or Cameroon. Obviously, their strength does not lie in their numbers. But somehow they have kept their faith and ethnicity longer than any other peoples in the world. Where today are the Assyrians and Babylonians and their gods? What has become of the Egyptian, Greek, or Roman gods? Miraculously the Jews have braved one holocaust after another, and the God of Abraham, Isaac, and Jacob is ours today.

And here is another amazing thought: by the middle of this century, for the first time in two thousand years, most of the world's Jews will be living in Israel.

More than most of us, Jews know how dark this world can be. Yet they know that a light shines in the darkness, and the darkness has not overcome it.

—ɷ—

Go ahead and busy yourself if you must with the decorating, the shopping, the worrying over small things that conceal larger matters. Pull out the punchbowl and the leaves for the table. After all, company is coming, company is coming.

Maybe you feel that it's the wrong time for Christmas. But it is the birth of the Savior, just the same.

The good news is that the one true God, the Almighty, knows we need a miracle. Christians and Jews alike attest to the *shema* found in Deuteronomy: "Hear, O Israel, the Lord our God is one . . ." The oneness, the singularity of God, is more than enough for us. He rebuilds what has been broken; relights what has gone out. It's miraculous, but this is how we too become children of light.

There is one light, one person who illuminates that darkness, one person who shines constantly after our resources are gone. There is only one, and we need only one.

The Douglas Fir

*T*he Douglas fir stands amid a hundred other firs just like it, on the Gearhart tree farm near Wolverine. Its branches are freighted with a little fresh snow; its evergreen needles feed, and its deep roots drink.

A generation ago, it was taken from a nursery and planted as a seedling among a great crowd. Once it was as tall as a person its age: at five years, and at ten years, and at fifteen years.

Now it is thirty years old, taller than any person but no taller than any other tree around it. In fact, it cannot be distinguished from other Douglas firs, unless its trunk is straighter or its branches stronger. When the heavy snow comes, its branches bend like any others. Its rings record the same weather.

Left here, this nameless tree would have a long life.

According to legend, Martin Luther was walking through the woods one clear night when all the stars gave him pause to think about the glory of the heavens that Christ had left for life on earth. He brought home a fir tree, set candles on it, and told his children that these lights were like the night stars, which Christ had left to come for us. Ever after, German children have decorated the Christmas tree, the *Tannenbaum,* just as all kinds of trees are decorated in other parts of the world—a eucalyptus tree in Madagascar, or a cactus in Mexico.

At night, when everyone else on the Gearhart farm is sleeping, the nameless Douglas fir stands under the night sky, and all the lights of heaven shine upon it.

—⁂—

Under another night sky, so the story goes, obscure shepherds tended to their work, which was lonely and paid little. Nothing much had happened to them before. Yet impossible news, glorious news, was about to be given to them, the least important people in the whole region. The angel did not announce it to the Governor of Palestine, did not announce it to King Herod, did not proclaim it to throngs in the markets, but brought it to these shepherds in the fields, and said, "For *to you* is born this day in the city of David a savior, who is Christ, the Lord."

To you!

And moreover, the angel said, "This shall be a sign *for you*: *you* shall find the baby wrapped in swaddling cloths and . . ." and I pause here—"and lying in a manger."

This humble child, this obscure child, lying in the least and lowliest place, was a King of Kings, Lord of Lords, a savior born for them.

In the gospel, the shepherds are nameless, but we know who they are. Since childhood we have worn their cloaks and imagined their emotions, and that child in a manger is our Christ, too.

—⟋⟋⟍—

Christmas trees have their fashions. Perhaps you recall the 1960s vogue for flocked or aluminum trees. The bushy Scotch pine was popular in the 1970s, until folks found that it didn't allow ornaments to hang properly and that it dropped its needles. Many tree farms are full of Scotch pines planted in those years. The lovely blue spruce drew admirers, who put up with its razor-sharp needles, but now it sells slowly. The white pine, while too weak to hold ornaments, makes an elegant wreath, as does the cedar; some prefer the balsam for its fragrance.

To get back to trees: shoppers have long found that the Douglas fir is reliable, but it has rarely been their first choice. The Fraser fir is this year's favorite. The "Cadillac of trees," it has a classic, Victorian silhouette, with soft, short, blue-and-silver needles. Accordingly, it's the most expensive. My local greenhouse doesn't have many left in stock.

They buy their trees from the Gearhart farm, which has been pruning and shaping trees all year, making them perfectly conical and protecting them from insects and wildlife. The Gearharts started cutting in September to ship trees all over the country— they brought in seasonal help and cut trees by the hundreds.

The Douglas fir was spared. There wasn't much demand for it; it could wait for another year, when it might be worth more money.

So there it stands, surrounded by dozens of other trees almost identical. It grows a little taller; its evergreen needles feed, its deep roots drink, and under the night sky it is blessed by a thousand nameless stars.

—ɯ—

Christ shared our world, shared our weather, shared our work, worries, and our joys; he grieved, and wept; he was tempted, and prayed; he shared our meals, our filth, our celebrations, our company. Maybe his back was a little straighter, his soul a little stronger; maybe he was much stronger, yet essentially he was so like us.

And that is where his concern lay, first and last. His profession was not to be a carpenter; not to be a teacher; but to be human. He came *for us*; he came *for you*.

—ɯ—

It turns out that demand for retail trees is high this year, for almost all varieties. Even in late November, large orders are being placed. One of the Gearhart family goes into the fields, to the back acres, and cuts down several dozen Douglas firs.

The fir rests in a crushing pile in the flat bed of a logging truck. Within a few days it goes through a bundler. Then it is shipped to a retail merchant, who leaves it bundled until many others have been sold; at last the strings are cut, it is put on display, and several days later a happy family buys this dying tree.

They set it down in a tree stand and give it its first drink of water in a month—like Christ on the cross, permitted to drink from a sponge of vinegar.

Perhaps, if you have purchased a Douglas fir, it is in your home today. It has given its life for you. You call it a Christmas tree; it could just as well stand for Good Friday.

Perhaps you regret that a tree has given its life for your brief pleasure.

But consider this: a few weeks ago, and for many years before it, it was nameless, obscure, living only to itself; except for one family with a proprietary interest, no one noticed it or cared for it. Now it will be loved, and dressed, and admired; it will give pleasure, and more than that, it will provide a witness of faith. When all the lights are burning tonight, it will remind a home of the glory Christ left and the light he brought to a darkened Earth.

This is how it is for all of us who are involved in the Christian life: whether we are shepherds, or carpenters, or freight drivers, or teachers, or merchants, or tree-cutters: we are involved in something greater than ourselves, and it gives our lives meaning. Christ showed us this. The truth of it echoes throughout our world.

Late tonight, when the snow falls gently on your roof, and all the stars are blessing your home, turn off the lights except for those on the tree.

Consider the life that Christ gave for you; consider the glory that Christ left to come to you; and let this silent Tannenbaum tell you the important news:

> *For to you is born this day in the city of David a savior,*
> *who is Christ, the Lord.*
> *And this shall be a sign for you;*
> *and this shall be a sign for you;*
> *and this shall be a sign for you.*

I'll Be Home for Christmas

*T*urn your crystal radio set back to the year 1943, and gather close to one another, because in a few moments, crackling across the airwaves, we will hear an important message.

That year was one of the longest years of the last century. Most have 365 days, but that had at least six hundred.

In that year alone, millions of Jews perished in the Holocaust. Hitler's armies occupied almost all of continental Europe; after months of heavy fighting, the Allies managed to regain North Africa and Sicily. England, pounded by bombs, was in desperate condition. Thousands of Americans waited there for the Allied invasion of Europe. For months they trained with broom handles and crude flight simulators, getting used to their British comrades, making friends with British civilians, as more and more Americans arrived. On December 10, General Dwight D. Eisenhower set up headquarters in England. His men didn't know it yet, but many would be landing at Normandy in just six months, while others would leave in just a few days for Anzio and some of the fiercest fighting of the war.

Just imagine what it was like to wait for that Christmas.

By now these men, some of them mere boys, had already been away from home longer than their fathers in the First World War. The lights had gone out all over Europe, and they were in the darkness. Each night, all of England went dark to make the job that much harder for German bombers.

Perhaps you remember those days. Perhaps you've heard your father or grandfather tell of them. But some experiences surpass words, such as that Christmas 1943, when so much was at stake, and home mattered so much, and folks back home first heard this haunting melody:

> *I'll be home for Christmas,*
> *you can count on me.*
> *Please have snow and mistletoe*
> *and presents on the tree.*
>
> *Christmas Eve will find me*
> *where the love-light gleams.*
> *I'll be home for Christmas,*
> *if only in my dreams.*[18]

—◊—

Have you been traveling this Christmas? Did you visit friends and family, and maybe a few other relatives and friends? Maybe you ventured out on snow-covered roads and asked for traveling mercies.

Being away from home is a tradition as old as Christmas itself.

The wise men, we are told, came from Persia, a journey of many weeks across treacherous terrain, and then found something even more treacherous at the court of King Herod. After they paid homage to the Christ child, they were warned in a dream not to return to Herod.

Similarly, Joseph had been told in a dream not to abandon Mary. Even after he brought her from Galilee to Bethlehem, a journey of many days, their travels were not done, for he was warned in yet another dream to flee with his family to Egypt:

An angel of the Lord appeared to Joseph in a dream and said, "Get up, take the child and his mother, and flee to Egypt, and remain there until I tell you; for Herod is about to search for the child, to destroy him." Then Joseph got up, took the child and his mother by night, and went to Egypt, and remained there until

the death of Herod. This was to fulfill what had been spoken by
the Lord through the prophet, "Out of Egypt I have called my
son." (Matthew 2:13–15)

This was the day after Christmas. After the scandal and mystery
of Mary's pregnancy, after the difficult journey late in her pregnancy, the bed in a barn, the strange visitors with their frightening
predictions . . . they could not even return home! They would have
to flee to Egypt, of all places, where their ancestors had once been
slaves.

Can you imagine how they longed for Galilee? How desperately
they waited for the next dream?

I'll be home for Christmas, if only in my dreams.

A lot of people have the notion that great faith is a plateau, a peaceful stillness, when more often it means leaving home. Starting with
Adam and Eve, everyone in the Bible leaves home. Noah builds an
ark. Hagar flees to the wilderness. Joseph is sold into slavery,
comes to prominence in Egypt, then brings his starving family
there. Generations later, when the Hebrews have fallen into slavery, Moses leads them out of Egypt. The young widow Ruth
accompanies her mother-in-law, saying, "Where you go, I will go;
where you lodge, I will lodge; your people shall be my people, and
your God my God" (Ruth 1:16, adapted). Even reluctant Jonah
eventually goes where God commands. Even the nation of Judah
is carried into exile in Babylon, where they recall the covenant
made with their father Abraham, "a wandering Aramean."

Which brings us to Christmas, and the day after Christmas.

That's when Mary and Joseph got the news that they must flee
to Egypt. For Joseph, it must have been terrible news. Back when
Mary turned up pregnant, his heart had broken; he had known such
a thing could happen to a young girl, yet he had wanted to dismiss
her quietly. What had stopped him was the angel. What kept them
together was the angel. And now the angel had come back to tell

them that they must pick up the child and their few belongings and run from Herod. The chairs in the workshop would remain unfinished. The basket of knitting would be abandoned.

Not a peaceful stillness, but a hasty flight marked the day after Christmas. Between the lines of the story we sense Mary and Joseph's deepening faith. They were in it all the way now. There was no getting out. With gracious and calm readiness, they did as the angel said and held their child tightly, for he would be their home. *Jesus would be their home.*

They continued on in the gospel promise that someday they would reach home, and in God's time they did—not just in a dream, but in waking reality:

> When Herod died, an angel of the Lord suddenly appeared in a dream to Joseph in Egypt and said, "Get up, take the child and his mother, and go to the land of Israel, for those who were seeking the child's life are dead." Then Joseph got up, took the child and his mother, and went to the land of Israel. But when he heard that Archelaus was ruling over Judea in place of his father Herod, he was afraid to go there. And after being warned in a dream, he went away to the district of Galilee. There he made his home in a town called Nazareth. (Matthew 2:19–23)

—⁂—

In 1943, two men named Gannon and Kent wrote "I'll Be Home for Christmas," one of the most moving songs of the whole war. It was a big hit for Bing Crosby—he took it to Number Three—and many others soon covered it. All over America it played, in bus terminals and train stations, in homes and in barracks. It played for those back home and for servicemen waiting to hear where they would go next.

Many who are too young to remember those poignant days know that song. It expresses something deeply and lastingly true about the holiday.

Perhaps you're not where you'd planned to be. You're tired of all life's dislocations and long to arrive somewhere, though it doesn't look like you will any time soon. Work and worry lie ahead as far as you can see. This Christmas will not approach the greeting card ideal. Yet your faith somehow keeps you going. Surprisingly you feel that God is with you. This strength sometimes carries you, and in such moments of calm and assurance it's possible to recall another Christmas years ago:

You are a child again, almost asleep in the back seat, watching the streetlights and shadows alternately overtake each other as a radio plays softly. You're miles from home, but in important sense, home is with you. Your father is driving, your mother watching the road, your older brother in the shadows beside you. The ride goes on and on; you succumb to its rising and falling and smooth endlessness. The road outlasts you, and at last you dream.

Getting the Hell Out

Drive through coal country in central Pennsylvania and you'll find Centralia. It's an older town with deep roots, which is part of the problem.

One day in 1962 there was a fire at the city landfill that wasn't fully doused. Through bad luck it spread underground, where it was harder to extinguish, and then it reached the veins of coal.

For years it went on, mostly out of sight. The townsfolk figured it would burn itself out, and even after the fire forced the mines to close, they pretended not to worry about it. By the 1970s, the air was filled with smoke and sulfur. Roads were hot and buckled and crumbling. Trees and grasses had been baked white, and volunteers had to put out the flames that erupted continually.

On Valentine's Day, 1981, twelve-year-old Todd Dombrowski and his cousin Eric were fixing a motorcycle in their grandmother's garage when Todd noticed smoke coming from the yard. He went to see if someone had thrown a cigarette into the leaves. All of a sudden, the ground gave way. He grabbed for some roots, screamed for Eric. As he said later, "It was real hot and it stank and it sounded like the wind was howling down there." If he had not grabbed onto a tree root, Todd would have been swallowed by a sinkhole more than 350 feet deep and 400 degrees Fahrenheit in temperature.

Two years later, large sections of Route 61 caved in.

The Office of Surface Mining, which had been studying the

Centralia fire for years, estimated that the only way to stop it was to dig it out, at a cost of $663 million. Instead, the U.S. Congress offered $42 million to buy out all the homes and businesses and move 1,100 people. The offer had a fifteen-year limit.

By 1991, most folks had chosen to go—but not everyone. A few holdouts suspected that this was a government plot to get their coal. They would stay in Centralia and fight it out in the courts, whatever it took.

You take Route 61 into Centralia today and find sidewalks, curbs, benches, driveways—but no houses. Well, maybe one survivor of a row of houses, now buttressed with bricks, and a few other dwellings here and there. In the hottest part of town, where the fire is closest to the surface, pipes vent noxious gases. Every street smells and tastes of sulfur.

Their town is a smoking hell, but forty-six people refuse to leave Centralia.

—m—

A man was begging at the Sheep Gate outside the Temple in Jerusalem—begging as he had every day for years—when Jesus came by. We understand that he had been an invalid for thirty-eight years. Perhaps he had the unhappy distinction of being the oldest beggar there.

Sheep came through this gate on the north side of the Holy City on their way to the nearby Temple, where they would be slaughtered, and in similar fashion invalids came here in droves to bathe in the pool said to have restorative powers. Now and then an underground spring percolated, which local superstition held was an angel stirring the waters to heal the first person who jumped in. Their hopes cruelly raised, the lame and blind raced each other to the waters, pushing aside those most in need of a cure, such as our old beggar.

It was a hellish situation, but Jesus happened by and discovered this man, learned how long he had been ill, and asked: "Do you want to be made well?"

This is the essential question posed by every doctor, therapist, or pastor. Some people, if they knew their own hearts, would have to say no. They are at home in hell.

We all are, at times. Every one of us has lain round that pool and complained, pretended that our problems were hopeless and let them become part of our identity. Certainly at times I have been the Oldest Beggar at the Sheep Gate.

We stay in situations gone bad, stubbornly believing they will someday be good again—painful love affairs, jobs that are killing us, marriages that have turned abusive. This stubbornness is a crazy kind of faith—quite literally crazy. We are not so far removed from the patients who cannot find their way out of a room once the furniture is rearranged.

Walter Jackson used to tell of a time he preached for the patients of a state hospital in Louisville. Some fastened their eyes on him intently, while others drifted off in caricatures of madness. His throat tight, Dr. Jackson spoke as best he could until a woman with wild hair stood up and shouted, "Go to hell! Go to hell! Go to hell!" Another patient responded, "Shut up! We're in hell! And he's trying to get us out of it!"

Here is a voice of sanity, speaking strange words: Jesus says, "I am the sheep gate. Whoever enters through me will be safe. They will go in and out, and find pasture. . . . I came that they might have life and have it abundantly" (John 10:7–10, adapted).

Abundant life is for all, but you have to go through the gate. You have to get up and get out of hell. The Oldest Beggar at the Sheep Gate did. After thirty-eight years, he had no need of his reverse celebrity. Perhaps he had no wife, no family, no job but begging, and wanted desperately to move about as freely as those passersby who took their health for granted. No one had inquired closely about his illness or regularly helped him into the supposedly healing waters. And then this stranger stopped to hear his story, listened with such feeling and concentration, and asked him a direct question.

The Oldest Beggar repeated it.

"Do I want to be made well?

"Are you for real?

"Listen, sir, I'm not from here, I was born in Bethsaida. My younger brother—he's nine years younger—grew up without me because of these legs. I couldn't help out, couldn't care for myself, fouled myself. After Mother died, Father made a pilgrimage and left me here so the Temple priests could take care of me. I'm sure he loved me, but he just didn't know what else to do. Well, none of their cures worked, so the priests just gave up on me. Maybe I am a sinful man—I don't know—but I believe in God, sir, and God can put things right. If someone would put me in the water, I'd be made well. I couldn't be there for my father when he died, or when my brother married, but someday his daughters will marry, and with all my soul I want to be able to stand and walk and dance with them."

That is just what Jesus told him to do.

Now in Jerusalem by the Sheep Gate there is a pool, called in Hebrew Beth-zatha, which has five porticoes. In these lay many invalids—blind, lame, and paralyzed. One man was there who had been ill for thirty-eight years. When Jesus saw him lying there and knew that he had been there a long time, he said to him, "Do you want to be made well?" The sick man answered him, "Sir, I have no one to put me into the pool when the water is stirred up; and while I am making my way, someone else steps down ahead of me." Jesus said to him, "Stand up, take your mat and walk." At once the man was made well, and he took up his mat and began to walk. (John 5:2–9)

A man who had been ill for thirty-eight years came into contact with the source of health, with life itself. You know what that is. That's heaven on earth.

—ᘛᘚ—

The people remaining in Centralia think that more should be done for them. When they met with their congressman a while back, the mayor demanded to know why the fire couldn't be put out. The congressman explained that digging it out would cost $662 million, and that to do this for forty-six people was more than even the government could justify.

Yet the Office of Surface Mining (OSM) put down a bed of clay near the church, at a cost of $100,000, because visibility there was so poor from heat and smoke. The OSM also used a backhoe to fill large holes with rocks, which soon resembled the lava rocks of a barbecue grill as blue flames erupted from them and set the brush and trees on fire.

At last, having determined that noxious gases and erosion threatened the lives of the remaining citizens of Centralia, the Commonwealth of Pennsylvania condemned their homes. The townspeople also went to court and charged that the government was taking their coal. One year later, Route 61 caved in again and closed indefinitely. The underground fire continued to spread, affecting 3,700 acres. Twice the county court ruled against the citizens; so did the state Supreme Court. But in 1997, Centralians celebrated the 125th anniversary of their hometown, and their mayor declared, "The borough will remain intact."

They still believed in a conspiracy to get their coal. They believed that the fire had moved out of town, even though recent tests had shown that the soil temperature was 400 degrees and that the fire was spreading.

One elderly resident said, "We just want to be left alone and to live out our lives in peace." A state official said, "I understand and sympathize with them. But there is a concern about the health and welfare of these people." On New Year's Eve, 1997, the fifteen-year offer to buy their homes expired.

—◊◊◊—

God has given you a New Year. What will you make of it? Another year just like the old one?

And who knows what the year will make of you? There may be all kinds of problems and dangers smoldering just below the surface. Hell keeps popping up in places that once were comfortable. If you think you may sit tight and have your life restored, you may wait a long, long time. Stubbornness is not the same as faithfulness.

Stay if you like; misery loves company. This man picked up his mat and walked.

Snow in Jerusalem

*J*erusalem is a holy city in three world religions. Jews pray at its Wailing Wall; Muslims at the golden Dome of the Rock; Christians upon the Mount of Olives. These and many other sacred spots have seen bitter fighting and the most irreligious violence.

Last Sunday, the people of Jerusalem woke up to snow. Nearly every year the city gets a trace of it, but usually it melts within an hour, so the little bit that remained until nightfall was a novelty.

That night, more than a foot of snow fell: it fell upon the Wailing Wall, upon the golden Dome of the Rock, upon the Mount of Olives. Snow fell on the Golan Heights, on the West Bank, and on every camp of soldiers in every disputed region.

In the morning, travel was paralyzed, almost all business was shut down, and strange dreams came true.

On this day, Israeli soldiers and Arab kids fought with snowballs and laughed as they did it. Today, for the Palestinian youth in their familiar red-and-white headgear, the *intifada* was completely harmless. In an east Jerusalem elementary school, the janitor put snow in a freezer so Palestinian kids from outside the city would get the chance to see it. And for this day, the building of Jewish settlements in the occupied territories ceased.

Children made snowmen and topped them with yarmulkes. An announcer on Channel 1 gleefully held up a handful of snow to show viewers what it looked like. One tourist said, "In the Bible, in the Psalms, when David says, 'white as snow,' I always

137

wondered how he knew what snow was like. Now I know." This same snow, mentioned in the Islamic and Christian scriptures, had fallen upon their holiest sites.

—⚬—

Before David made it the capital of his kingdom, Jerusalem was a small and ancient town. It had belonged to the Jebusites until Joshua had captured it, but in settling the country, the Israelites had left the town in Jebusite hands, and it had remained a small town until David recaptured it about 1000 BCE.

The terrain offered few advantages for defense or farming. Ironically, David chose Jerusalem as his capital because it had belonged to Gentiles and so was independent of the twelve rival tribes of Israelites. In other words, it was a neutral site, a compromise.

Here, at this crossroads of cultures, David brought the ark of the covenant and established a tabernacle where foreigners had worshiped foreign gods. Within a generation this unlikely place became the center of Israel, the City of David, a holy city, which the prophet Ezekiel could imagine "in the center of the nations, with countries all around her." Renaissance cartographers placed Jerusalem in the center of world maps, and indeed the city has occupied a central place in the world's imagination. The Israeli writer Amos Elon calls Jerusalem "the capital of memory." In some senses it is the capital of the world.

—ᚱ—

Indeed, three world religions cannot forget their sins because Jerusalem stands as a reproach.

Even though the city's golden walls are bathed in light, we cannot quite forget that the Hebrews slaughtered the ancient people of Palestine in occupying their promised land; or that the modern state of Israel has occupied lands and oppressed Palestinians without apology. We cannot forget that when Muslims conquered cities, they turned churches into mosques, or that when they conquered Jerusalem they built the Dome of the Rock right where the Great Temple had stood—clearly meaning that Islam superseded those faiths. We cannot forget that Christians burned not only Muslims and Jews, but even one another.

Rouen, Cairo, Riyadh, Bethlehem, Belfast, and Selma all belong to the country of religious violence whose capital is Jerusalem.

In Jesus' time, Jerusalem seethed with Jewish rebellion against the Romans. If faithlessness had led to the city's fall before, some of them now were determined to save it with their fanaticism. A sect called the Zealots led raids in the hills, and another called the Sicarii carried out terror in the streets against fellow Jews suspected of collaboration. Jesus, the confrontational but nonviolent Christ, cried:

> "Jerusalem, Jerusalem, the city that kills the prophets and stones those who are sent to it! How often have I desired to gather your children together as a hen gathers her brood under her wings, and you were not willing! See, your house is left to you." (Luke 13:34–35)

Days before his death, as he entered the holy city in seeming triumph, he wept over it:

"If you, even you, had only recognized on this day the things that make for peace! But now they are hidden from your eyes." (Luke 19:42)

It was supposed to be the earthly dwelling place of God, a witness to the world. Instead it is a place of terrible and divine irony. Maybe the horrible drama is God's way of shaming our religions before the world, of announcing: *All three of you—you do not possess me; I possess you. You were charged to bless my people, all my people. It is not such a hard thing to do. Even people who know nothing of me have done it. And if you will not bless my people, then the world will find that you are a curse. Generations will fall away from you, faithful people will shun you, but they will not fall from me, for I have made them and they are mine.*

—ɯ—

Or perhaps God, in his infinite grace, continues to bless this place in spite of itself, just as he blesses all of us. Perhaps Jerusalem stands for the universal need of grace, and that may be why this week God saw fit to relieve the ironies of his holy city. "Though your sins are like scarlet, they shall be like snow" (Isaiah 1:18).

Thousands of people, real people you and I may know, could not live without God's grace. I am thinking of my friend Barry, who moved to Israel after we finished college, hoping to live out his rediscovered faith. He found to his disillusionment that the country was less democratic than advertised. He also found the Palestinians less than sympathetic, given their share of the violence. Friends and family pleaded with him to return. Barry chose to stay. "I know it's not for everybody," he said, "but it's for me. People in the States think they're insulated from these troubles, but they're not. I figure if I'm going to live as a Jew, I might as well be here."

Barry and his wife just had a child, their first, a son. Although it troubles him sometimes to have his family in such an environment, this is where God has blessed him with a wife and now a child. In Jerusalem, typical blessings cannot be taken for granted. Most mornings he shops pleasantly in an Arab grocery. His wife (who is French) and their neighbors (Moroccan) communicate in an ancient language (Hebrew) that elsewhere is dead. He meets people from all over the world in the very places where the twelve tribes of Israel lived alongside Amorites and Hittites. These things matter all the more when a bus explodes in the street and destroys the so-called peace process.

Barry and others of three religions live out their scriptures in this day. Like the psalmists thousands of years ago, they know God's power to comfort or make us uncomfortable:

> Praise the LORD, O Jerusalem!
> Praise your God, O Zion!
> For he strengthens the bars of your gates;
> he blesses your children within you.
> He grants peace within your borders;
> he fills you with the finest of wheat.
> He sends out his command to the earth;
> his word runs swiftly.
> He gives snow like wool;
> he scatters frost like ashes.
> He hurls down hail like crumbs—
> who can stand before his cold?
> (Psalm 147:12–17)

What God may do next no one can predict—who can stand before his cold?—but this week at least has been a gracious departure from Jerusalem's usual climate.

When the snow melts and children start throwing rocks again, we may take some comfort in being half a world away, but we should not be too comfortable. Divided Jerusalem is a symbol for all religious failure, whether in Ohio, South Carolina, or County Clare. That is why Jerusalem really is the capital city of the world. Lest we forget, Psalm 122 reminds us to "pray for the peace of Jerusalem."

One Hundred Tons of Ice

*I*t's the least valuable thing up north. We have to pay people to move it out of the way. It's a nuisance. We salt it down, break it up, shovel it out. Some folks don't even like ice in their tea, they see so much of it in winter. But almost a hundred and seventy years ago, one man saw an opportunity where we see just ice.

He was Frederic Tudor, a Boston merchant who pioneered its transport and became known as the Ice King. The idea had come to him at a family gathering when his older brother had idly mused that Massachusetts ice might be quite a commodity in the tropics. Frederic soon took his first shipments to the Caribbean, sold it cheaply, and built a market. He teamed up with a supplier who provided ice with very few impurities, cut in blocks of uniform size from a spring-fed pond. He found that packing his ice in sawdust decreased melting losses from two-thirds to almost nothing.

Once he had perfected his methods, he turned his eye to the most remote and sweltering place he could think of: Calcutta, India.

In 1833, in Calcutta, if you wanted ice, you had to settle for an inferior product made forty miles upriver, at Hooghly. There, at a small ice factory, water was left overnight in clay pots and cooled with saltpeter; in the morning, a little skin of ice was skimmed from the surface. It was sort of slushy—in fact it was called Hooghly slush—and it was available only part of the year.

In the late spring of 1833, Tudor supervised the loading of the ship *Tuscany* to his exact specifications. Down in the hull, he had

workers install a sheathing of boards, then six inches of straw at the bottom and sides, then boards again, then a foot of straw all around, then more boards, then about twenty inches of straw all around. He expected to lose about a third of the ice during the three-month journey.

On the twelfth of May, the *Tuscany* left Charlestown, Rhode Island, with one hundred and eighty tons of ice. The ship's Captain Littlefield was well aware of the historic nature of his voyage. He recorded the moment that his cargo became "the first ice to cross the equator."

The ship sailed in the heat of summer, and the captain must have been anxious that this freight would survive the journey. On September 10, with a clear and proud hand, he wrote in his log: "We have arrived in Calcutta with one hundred tons of ice."

What a scene in Calcutta that day! It was as if a new world had opened up to the millions there who had never imagined such luxury. One eyewitness wrote:

How many Calcutta tables glittered that morning with ice! The butter dishes were filled; the goblets of water were converted into miniature Arctic seas with icebergs floating to the surface. All business was suspended until noon, that people might rush about to pay each other congratulatory visits.[19]

The benefits of this ice went far beyond cooling butter and tea. It kept food fresh for weeks (something unheard-of) and helped doctors in the treatment of fevers.

It was incredible—that something so worthless in New England might be so valuable in Calcutta.

—ൡ—

What kind of people did Jesus call for his disciples? And what did they have to offer?

Think of the commonest folk imaginable, people who might just have stepped off the number seven bus, seated around a charismatic man who told them:

"You are the light of the world. A city built on a hill cannot be hid. No one after lighting a lamp puts it under a bushel, but on a stand, so that it gives light to the whole house. Let your light so shine before others that they may see your good works and give glory to your father in heaven." (Matthew 5:14–16, adapted)

Jesus didn't say this about himself. He said this about them— about us. Ordinary people held a high place in his estimation. Despite their questions, doubts, and fears, they got his message; indeed, they followed him in great crowds and eventually resembled an army. Ordinary people still get the gospel, so far as anyone can.

But we don't always esteem ourselves as he did. The roller-rink church organ makes us wince, the wobbly voices in the choir make us giggle, and even as the student pastor raises a hand in benediction, we have to stifle a suspicion that we're really not useful to Jesus. Believe it or not, we are.

According to the Sermon on the Mount, we are the light of the world. Long before the gospels were written, ordinary people remembered his words and told others what they had heard. That's still how it happens—how the gospel happens.

—∿∿—

You don't have to go all the way to Calcutta to find a use for ice. Years ago, folks did it right here. Workers on the Little Traverse Bay would cut a path of open water to protect the docks from the ice, and a conveyor belt would load the blocks onto wagons. Icemen in rubber aprons were able to lift one-hundred-pound blocks with just a pair of tongs.

These weren't particularly unusual folks—they were just as common as your neighbors. Harold Hahn used to cut ice on the bay with a gas-powered rotary blade. Ed Jullieret cut and stored ice for keeping fish in his restaurant. Guy Engles had an icehouse, too, for commercial use, and in the summertime he would load a drayfull for delivery out on the Point.

These folks knew where to look for something worthwhile. Don't imagine that they were looking anywhere you never saw before. No, they just had discovered the practical application of a gospel truth—that every one of us, and everything, is useful to God.

You know, people get rich not by finding gold or diamonds, but by figuring out what to do with a hundred tons of ice. People discover their real worth by giving that to Christ and seeing the wonders it can do.

Just think what you have to give to the general renewal of this church. For example, you may have children. Maybe you don't even particularly like children; you just happen to have some hundred tons of them and don't mind sharing them on Sundays. Well, it just so happens that quantity counts, and by bringing your own kids you can encourage others to show up.

Maybe you have a crate full of glassware left over from Aunt Sally's. There should be a church rummage sale soon. Someone else will have the glasses, and the church will have five dollars, which buys about twenty lunches in Haiti.

You might have nothing else to bring this church but your cheerfulness. It might not seem like much to you, but good nature is precious here.

Everybody has a few doubts, and you might have a ton of them. Maybe you thought a church could never use your doubts. It just so happens that the adult Sunday school class really needs you to voice them and start a discussion to make them examine their faith. Once you have unburdened those doubts, who knows? Your own faith might surface.

Maybe all you can bring is something broken—a broken heart, broken home, broken marriage. That's how you bear witness to the sustaining grace of Christ.

Or perhaps you've had a terrible experience in your life, and it's taken all these years for you to put it mostly out of mind. Well, someone else may be going through a similar situation now, someone who could be helped by your story. For the first time in years you might be able to use that pain. God's uses are like that: redemptive.

—៳—

In the heat of the summer, there is nothing better than a cool glass of—anything. Just rubbing the glass against your face gives some relief. It is a measure of the comfort we take for granted that today, even in Calcutta, you can find an ice-cold Pepsi.

To all of us sharing this broad sun, Christ says—and you can believe him or not—*you are the light of the world.*

The sun's rays are strong, but way down deep in the hold of your ship, underneath all the sawdust, you are carrying a precious commodity, and when it is brought above decks it will glitter and shine and throw back the light of the sun.

For Christ's sake, carry it to its destination.

Spring
—⟋⟍—

Seed Catalog

*I*f you trust the Farmers' Almanac, this is the season for planting. The stores are full of gardening supplies and mailboxes are full of seed catalogs. We've gotten quite a few at our house, including one from Burpee Seeds, a company that brought me to my knees when I was only ten.

There are few things as satisfying as spending time on our knees, hands deep in dirt, working a bed of delphiniums, marigolds, impatiens. Or snapbeans, sweetcorn, rutabagas, pumpkins, herbs of every kind. Over at Bluff Gardens, Sophy Carpenter and her crew have been planting since March, when they put parsley, cabbage, cauliflower, and peppers in the greenhouse. Outside, asparagus should be coming up now. Next week they'll put in peas, potatoes, beets, carrots, lettuce, and spinach. And up near Levering Road, Gretchen and Joseph Van Loozen are putting in seedlings with their son Gabe, who has been able to name every flower and vegetable in the garden since the age of six.

These people know their business. God, on the other hand, appears to be a hopeful but careless and inefficient gardener. Sometimes his word takes root and sometimes it doesn't. In the remarkable thirteenth chapter of Matthew's gospel, we find Jesus preaching in the open air to a crowd gathered on the fertile land near a lakeshore, perhaps because the synagogues don't welcome him any longer. It's a defiant message, perfect for the setting, and Jesus states his challenge in the very first word:

149

"Listen!" he said. "A sower went out to sow; and as he sowed, some seed fell by the wayside; and the birds came and devoured it. Some fell upon stony ground, where there was no depth of soil; it sprang up instantly, but when the sun rose it was scorched, for it had no roots. Other seed fell among thorns, and the thorns came up and choked the life out of it. But others fell upon good ground, and yielded fruit, some a hundred-fold, some sixty-fold, others thirty-fold. Whoever has ears to hear, let them hear." (Matthew 13:3–9)

You can almost hear the restive stirring of his audience: Is he talking about us? Throughout this thirteenth chapter, Jesus speaks in parables about arable land and uncomprehending people. Here at the close of the first parable, he offers a challenge: "Those who have ears to hear, let them hear!"

The disciples aren't sure what the parable means, ironically enough. So he explains what happens to the various seeds of faith (Matthew 13:18–23). At times we receive God's word in stony silence, at other times eagerly but with no real depth; lesser concerns can crowd out that word; and then—surprise!—some particle of faith grows and yields far more than we have ever expected.

I can understand the disciples' confusion. Frankly, I'm not sure what this parable means, either, except that Jesus scatters his word inefficiently, indiscriminately, to unpromising places and people. Talk about Christian broadcasting!

Apparently God will go to some foolish extremes to spread his word and see if we will listen.

According to the Creation story, God formed humankind out of *adam*, the earth, breathed life into it, and then let come what may. Jesus' parable is another such creation story. We are clay, turned-up soil, and out of such humble beginnings, Jesus means to raise something. Call it the new life, a life in Christ, but this life starts with our listening. His word is the seed, and we are the crop. What he is growing is *us*.

—〰—

The people who heard Jesus preach out-of-doors had come for a variety of reasons. Some, I suppose, came just because of the curiosity of the thing. Others because he was notorious and they meant to catch him in blasphemy. Others because he had gained a reputation as a wonder-worker—they came more for what he might *do* than what he might *say*.

And some, I suppose, came because they weren't satisfied with their lives and were ready to hear a word about a new life. They had followed the usual promises to the usual trouble: women who had traded on their looks, men who had made shady deals, parents who had lost the respect of their children, people who had been brought to their knees. These indeed were the people Jesus hoped to reach.

Miraculously his word had come to them—not to the proud or pious, but to them, and on the spot they began to grow. Jesus speaks of it just a few verses later in this same thirteenth chapter of Matthew:

> "The kingdom of heaven is like a grain of mustard seed, which a man took and sowed in his field. It is the smallest of seeds, and yet, when it has grown, it is the greatest of herbs, and it becomes a great tree, so that the birds of the air come and nest in its branches." (Matthew 13:31–32)

Maybe God *does* know his business. Maybe he *does* know how to grow things. We know all about efficiency; we are, let us proudly admit, the best farmers, no, *agricultural engineers* the world has ever known. But we don't know beans about how the gospel grows or where it might take root.

One after the other in this remarkable chapter, we hear stories about wheat and tares, yeast and flour, a treasure hidden in a field—parables about listening, understanding, and establishing the kingdom of God.

At this point, God's foolishness is absolutely breathtaking. God is leaving the ultimate goal of his creation up to us. His word is the seed, and we are the crop. What he is growing is the *kingdom of God* through the work of Gretchen, Joseph and Sophy.

When I was ten I saw an ad in *Boys' Life* magazine promising, or seeming to promise, big money from selling Burpee Seeds. I wasn't very good at it. Over and over I trudged the neighborhood with sample packets and a catalog, but about all I got was advice to try earlier the next spring. A budding capitalist brought to his knees.

There were packets of cucumber, carrot, daisy, nasturtium, hyacinth, peppers. . . . What would a boy do with all those seeds? Well, I dumped them in a culvert a couple of blocks from home. Amazingly, they grew into a riot of vegetables and flowers. The culvert apparently held rainwater and the seeds worked into the soil. You never know.

Nowadays when I preach, maybe only a handful really listen, listen with their spines and shoulder blades. And yet I can see the results, new life getting started, the kingdom of God coming up.

Over the years, I've learned why some people really listen on Sundays and some people don't. If you're entirely satisfied with your present life, you're not going to be much interested in a new one. Your ears will not be open to the word of life that might fall into them. Only if you've been broken up, turned over, tilled and even fertilized will you really receive this new life. The smooth hard road where streams of people pass is no place for it to grow.

Which brings us back to Gretchen, Joseph, Sophy, people who will pray for us, get down on their knees for us, and prepare us to receive the word of God. Someone has to break us up a little, so that God's new life might grow. Part of God's apparent foolishness is to assign us this work of prayer.

Have you ever been prayed for by Joseph or Gretchen? Have you seen their eyes close during worship at our time of joys and concerns? Have you perhaps gotten canned vegetables from Sophy after coming home from the hospital? They are not proselytizers, by any stretch, but it's because of their regular, gentle concern that ordinary, unlikely people receive the word of God. Some of Gretchen's admittedly raffish friends would never set foot in a church, but they already know the love of God by her kindness and her prayer. And when his friends need to hear something, Joseph has a gentle, candid way of getting his digs in.

Jesus said, "The harvest is plentiful, but the workers are few." He was talking not about a hobby, but a life's work. You can see the kingdom come up if you're willing to get your hands dirty and spend some time on your knees.

Hip-Deep

*T*he grass is sweet at Bonnie and Gordon Oswalt's farm. Earlier this spring, the ewes were brought in from the pastures where they had wintered (they're healthier if wintered out-of-doors). They were sheared so they could be cool and comfortable in the barns and so the Oswalts could watch them closely as they lambed, and they were fed the second cutting, that is the best cutting of hay, molasses for energy, and mineral blocks high in salt and selenium.

Gordon and Bonnie keep five hundred ewes, and are on pace for eight hundred to a thousand lambs. It has been a good year— muddy, but productive. Each lamb has been tagged, cataloged, color-coded by barn, and numbered. A lamb has the same number as its mother so if they get separated, Bonnie or the grandkids can reunite them.

And what a sight are the lambs! Such a stiff-legged gait, with such top-heavy heads! In these fragile early days, they stay close to the ewes, but soon they'll be in the fields with the other lambs, frolicking like comics, and by September they'll be weaned.

—◊—

Jesus came from farm county known for its green hills, lakes, and pastureland. You can imagine how the psalms spoke to him:

154

The LORD is my shepherd; I shall not want.
He makes me lie down in green pastures;
he leads me beside still waters;
    he restores my soul.

(Psalm 23:1–3)

The prophet Ezekiel had pictured God as a good shepherd who would seek out his scattered flock, bring them to good pastureland, and would feed them with justice (Ezekiel 34). Jesus' own words echoed this imagery. He said, *I am the good shepherd.* He had come for *the lost sheep of Israel,* and would leave ninety-nine to find one that was lost.

Which brings us to the story of how Jesus appeared to Simon Peter and four other disciples who had been fishing all night on the Sea of Galilee. He had appeared to them just this way three years before, when he had called them. Now he had returned for them from the dead. Their dumbstruck awe, their silly love, must have surpassed words. Simon Peter was so moved at the sight of him that he swam to shore.

Remember that Jesus had once chosen Simon as the chief apostle, had named him Peter, or the Rock, for his strength and stability; yet on the night of Jesus' arrest, this Peter had denied him three times.

Now Jesus asked him a direct question: "Simon, son of John, do you love me?" Note that he no longer called him Peter. Simon said, "Yes, Lord, you know that I love you." Jesus asked him again, "Simon, son of John, do you love me?" Peter swore that he did. And when Jesus asked a third time, Peter must have remembered his three denials, for he grew anxious, and well he should have. Jesus wanted more than words; he wanted Simon Peter to prove it. He said, "Feed my sheep."

When they had finished breakfast, Jesus said to Simon Peter, "Simon son of John, do you love me more than these?" He said to him, "Yes, Lord; you know that I love you." Jesus said to him, "Feed my lambs." A second time he said to him, "Simon son of John, do you love me?" He said to him, "Yes, Lord; you know that I love you." Jesus said to him, "Tend my sheep." He said to him the third time, "Simon son of John, do you love me?" Peter felt hurt because he had said to him the third time, "Do you love me?" And he said to him, "Lord, you know everything; you know that I love you." Jesus said to him, "Feed my sheep." (John 21:15–17)

We are all in ministry. When Jesus said, "Feed my sheep," he meant us—you and me. This is part of the miracle of the resurrection—that Jesus rose in all his power and then entrusted us, in all our weakness, to be the Christ.

You, here. Have you ever thought about being in ministry?

Are you baptized? Then you already are.

Have you been feeding any of Jesus' sheep?

You'll want to try on a pair of boots, seeing as it's been a muddy spring and sheep aren't the cleanest animals.

Now just cradle this lamb in your arms like a baby. Go ahead and take its bottle, too. You see that its tail has already been cut. This lamb and its mother started out in a private pen in the barn; then they shared a larger pen with a few other families, and after three or four days, they were let out into the pasture. Gordon has planted a mix of grasses to provide a balance of nutrients. Each acre of land can support six to eight ewes plus their lambs; the sheep graze it right down to the roots, and move on to another pasture.

Isn't that a special bond? The lamb feels so warm and close. This is what it feels like to be in ministry. Even when you're hip-deep in sheep dip, it's a wonderful experience.

We don't like to think of ourselves or other people as sheep. It's not flattering. In truth, the sheep of Palestine were intelligent and could be led by the sound of a shepherd's voice. Yet they were inescapably needy, and so are we. The old words are true: *All we like sheep have gone astray.*

We are either suckling, or weaning, or grazing: suckling the milk of faith, or weaning away from platitudes to ask the hard questions, or grazing in the rich and fertile scriptures. These are the stages of Christian life. Everyone passes through them, and seeing that folks do so successfully is the work of a church.

Like it or not, we merit some unflattering comparisons. The finance committee knows that a church can graze the pasture right down to the roots. Sometimes the pastor stands hip-deep in sheep dip.

And then there are sacrificial lambs. They have always been part of religious life. They were slaughtered at Passover while the Temple authorities, without a sense of irony, were prosecuting Jesus. Today is no different; when things go wrong, the knives come out.

Like Simon Peter, who was entrusted with much, and entrusted with it again, you and I have much to answer for. Our local church has so much potential, and it will never realize it until we realize our own. True, some circumstances will not be to your liking. To get your work done you may need a pair of tall boots. Sometimes, when no else is doing what you know needs to be done, you will have to do it. Not only does the church need that of you—Jesus expects that of you.

Think of how many times we have chosen not to do so. Think how many times we have denied Jesus! And still he entrusts us with his ministry; still he asks, "Do you love me?"

Just open your arms to the Beams' nine-year-old daughter, Melissa. This is what it feels like to be in ministry.

Your lovely, loving, needful church has been called in spite of itself. Has it been easy? Has it been without costs or discomforts? No, of course not. Yet you can feel those in your care, warm and close: some suckling . . . some weaning . . . and some grazing . . .

Such as Mabel Hawkins here, ninety-three years young, who has long been grazing in the fertile scriptures.

This is what it feels like to be in ministry. Pastors and laypeople alike, we are hip-deep in our own guilt and shortcomings, yet called to be Christ to others.

Two weeks later, two thousand years later, we can still experience Easter, still say, *Yes, Lord, you know I love you,* and find that the risen Christ has placed a living creature of God in our arms.

Here Today

On an autumn day in 1813, John James Audubon was traveling along the Ohio River from Henderson, Kentucky, to Louisville, fifty-five miles away. It was noontime. But all at once the skies grew dark beneath a vast cloud of birds migrating south, an immense and swiftly moving flock. They stretched as far north, east, and west as he could see, actually shutting out the light of the sun, and when a hawk approached, they maneuvered instantly, twisting and wheeling, all in perfect formation, at sixty miles an hour.

Figuring two birds to the square yard, he estimated that by the time he reached Louisville, one billion birds had crossed the Ohio River. Still the migration was not over; it continued three full days.

Audubon had seen these birds before—every American had. And what he saw inspired him to pursue his career of painting and cataloging birds. What were they?

Passenger pigeons, the most plentiful birds in the world. They made up 40 percent of the birds of North America. Some would also say they were the finest birds on the continent. Audubon's portrait notes the regal posture; the small head and neck and massive breast muscles; the long, pointed wings and tail. They had beautiful plumage—a color ranging from blue to slate blue—and bright red eyes.

Fortunately for farmers, they did little damage to crops, preferring to eat beechnuts and chestnuts and worms and insects. They nestled in the very tops of trees, cooing softly in breeding season, otherwise calling *kee-kee-kee* in flocks so large that they could be heard four or five miles away.

Of all domestic birds, they were the strongest and most agile. Passenger pigeons flew great distances, a hundred miles sometimes, in search of food. But the muscular breasts that made them such tremendous flyers also made them good eating—and restaurants in the cities paid big money, twenty cents a bird. It was said they tasted better than chicken. It was said that they fattened hogs faster than seed corn. At first casual hunters fired indiscriminately at the huge clouds of pigeons, dropping half-a-dozen with a single shotgun blast. In time, professional hunters would develop far more mercenary methods to take pigeons in huge quantities.

These men would fashion a live decoy by sewing a bird's eyes shut and tethering it to a stool; they called this a "stool pigeon." When other pigeons swooped down from the treetops, the hunters caught them in nets.

In the spring of 1878, when the fields were bare but a foot of snow still lay in the woods, the largest flock ever seen settled right here where I live in northern Michigan. For a hundred square miles, every tree of every size was filled with birds. Word went out across the telegraph wires and drew five hundred full-time pigeon hunters. They spread salt on the ground and trapped the pigeons under nets. They tricked them to the ground with stool pigeons, netted them, and crushed their skulls. They fired shotguns for hours—there was no need to aim—and stopped only when they grew tired of retrieving carcasses. That year they shipped by rail from here millions of dead birds.

God help us, we were created in the image of God, and we sometimes imagine that the kingdom of God belongs to us. We call land "real estate," claim it as our own, and name our developments after what we have cleared away—crowded places with names like Chippewa Hills, Fox Run, Quail Hollow. There are no fox in Fox Run. There are no quail in Quail Hollow. Not far from where I live, there's a bulldozed work-in-progress called, ironically, The Preserve. From time to time we note that some species are reduced, and we recognize that our expansion means that something else will have to give—but we really do not think about it all that much.

They were here yesterday. We are here today. We have all but accepted that many of them will be gone tomorrow.

It is true that Jesus noted, "Two sparrows are sold for a penny," and counseled, "Do not be afraid; you are of more value than many sparrows." Yet as the old song has it, God's eye is on the sparrow. And if he favors his creatures the way he does the poor, then maybe we should keep an eye on the sparrow, too. As the psalmist said, anticipating the kingdom of God,

> Even the sparrow finds a home, and the swallow a nest for herself, where she may lay her young, at your altars, O LORD of hosts, my King and my God. Happy are those who live in your house, ever singing your praise. (Psalm 84:3–4)

There is still room enough for wild animals and people to coexist, but there is no room for carelessness.

Perhaps we take the earth for granted because deep in our hearts we think that we will have it forever. We are like the rich fool who forgot that one day he would have to return all that God had given him: "God said to him, 'You fool! This very night your life is being demanded of you. And the things you have prepared, whose will they be?'" (Luke 12:20).

We would do well to consider the least modern of saints, St. Francis of Assisi. Born into wealth, he gladly sacrificed it all for a chosen life of simplicity and poverty: begging meals, sleeping in caves and ditches, not worrying about what God would provide. "Look at the birds of the air," Jesus had said, "they neither sow nor reap nor gather into barns, and yet your heavenly father feeds them." St. Francis was determined to prove that an eminently practical and sane way to live.

All God's creatures were his company. He spoke of lambs, cattle, and horses as his brothers and sisters, and tradition tells us that he preached to the birds.

—ɯ—

In 1857, a committee reported on a game bill to the State Legislature of Ohio:

> The passenger pigeon needs no protection. Wonderfully prolific, having the vast forests of the north as its breeding grounds, it is here today, and elsewhere tomorrow; and no ordinary destruction can lessen them . . .[20]

In fact, they began to disappear at an alarming rate, and the last sizable nesting in Michigan was seen in 1881. As the nineteenth century came to a close, conservationists weren't sure the pigeons still existed. One bird-watching organization offered a reward for a freshly killed pigeon, until it realized that such an incentive might really finish the species off. In 1900, a small boy in Pike County, Ohio, using a BB gun he had just gotten for Christmas, killed the last passenger pigeon seen in the wild.

Soon the only survivor belonged to the Cincinnati Zoo, a female named Martha. She could not put her powerful wings and muscles to use and fly more than ten feet. She died on September 1, 1914, almost one hundred years to the day since John James Audubon had seen a flock of pigeons cross the Ohio.

Just a few decades before, they had been the most numerous birds on earth—billions of them! So many that they had darkened the skies! And now they were extinct.

One man wrote:

> The reduction of this once abundant bird to absolute extermination by man's greed should be a lesson to us all, and stifle all opposition to the efforts now being made by national and state governments on behalf of other birds threatened with a like fate. What is the loss of a little sport to us, compared with the extinction of a wild species—something that the hand of man can never replace?[21]

Passenger pigeons were hunted to extinction right where I live. They nested in tamarack trees. I live in a subdivision called Tamarack Trails. There are no tamaracks in Tamarack Trails. And, honestly, sometimes when local traffic stops so wild turkeys can cross the road, I find it a bother.

We are always building, building, building—everything but the kingdom of God. I do not believe that it will be God's kingdom if we have swept other beings from it. We have an obligation to return God's world to him intact, and surely he's watching. His eye is on the sparrow. And I know he watches me.

The Holy Grail

*I*n the year 1100, Jerusalem belonged to the Moors, or Muslims, and Christians throughout Europe burned with indignation at the thought. Over the next one hundred and fifty years they would set out on no less than seven Crusades to recover the holy lands and holy artifacts.

Among them were the Knights Templar, who wore coats of white with red crosses to signify that they were most devout and pure. Devoutly they murdered many Moors and plundered the ancient city of Constantinople, recovering (so they said) Christ's crown of thorns and the Holy Rood, or true cross of Christ. At Antioch they discovered the lance that had pierced his side, and elsewhere they claimed to have found the bloody sword that had cut off the head of John the Baptist.

Most fervently of all, they searched for the Holy Grail. Legend said that Jesus had blessed this cup at the Last Supper; that Joseph of Arimathea had collected the precious blood of Christ in it; and that years later, Joseph had brought it to Britain, to a town called Glastonbury. Now, in these evil times, it had disappeared. Some said that it had been taken up to heaven and was now a phantom, a vision; that it could be seen only by the pure of heart through prayer and fasting. Others said that it was real and solid, a treasure waiting to be found.

During this time of the Crusades, the legends of King Arthur grew popular, tales that reflected both these traditions of the Grail.

Sometimes the Round Table knights sought a solid Grail; sometimes, like Sir Galahad, they caught a vision of it.

What did it look like? Well, it was said to be made of gold and silver and encrusted with precious gems. It was said to have magical, healing powers, that it could save you from death.

Now, you may not believe this, but there are people yet today searching for the Holy Grail. Modern-day descendants of the Knights Templar who call themselves the Keepers of the Grail believe that it may be in an abbey in Scotland. Abbots in Glastonbury, England, believe that when their original abbey was destroyed, the monks escaped with the Grail brought by Joseph of Arimathea. This chalice, known as the Nanteos Cup, is a humble vessel of a common alloy.

Another, more spectacular chalice, encrusted with jewels, resides in a museum in Dublin. Other Christians in Constantinople suggest that the Grail may belong to the vast collections of the Orthodox Holy See.

In fact, on the Internet you will find hundreds of pages and dozens of possibilities. It is possible to go Web searching for the Holy Grail.

—∿—

If we want to find the Holy Grail, we might as well go back to the very beginning, to the earliest document about the Lord's Supper. Paul's first letter to the Corinthians was written by the year 50 CE, before any of the gospels. Amazingly, within two decades of Jesus' death, the sacrament was exactly as we know it today:

> For I received from the Lord what I also handed on to you, that the Lord Jesus on the night when he was betrayed took a loaf of bread, and when he had given thanks, he broke it and said, "This is my body that is for you. Do this in remembrance of me." In the same way he took the cup also, after supper, saying, "This cup is the new covenant in my blood. Do this, as often as you drink it, in remembrance of me." For as often as you eat this

bread and drink the cup, you proclaim the Lord's death until he comes. (1 Corinthians 11:23–26)

Maybe Christians understood the Lord's Supper so early and so completely because Jesus had shared meals with countless friends and strangers, and had shown in these meals how generous God could be. The Lord's Supper is a foretaste of a heavenly banquet; the first taste of the kingdom of God. Like the other sacrament recognized by all Christendom, the sacrament of baptism, it manifests the presence of God, the kingdom come into our lives.

Let me say this again: the kingdom is come. Jesus announced it with one word, a simple preposition. In the original Greek of Luke's gospel, the word is *entos,* which can mean either within or among. He said, "The kingdom of God is *entos*":

Once Jesus was asked by the Pharisees when the kingdom of God was coming, and he answered, "The kingdom of God is not coming with things that can be observed; nor will they say, 'Look, here it is!' or 'There it is!' For, in fact, the kingdom of God is among you." (Luke 17:20–21)

This day Christians all over the world, of every sect and denomination, however and wherever they worship, will share one unifying and satisfying meal dating back to the dawn of our faith, to an hour, a specific hour, when Jesus was still alive. He broke bread at a Passover and transformed that holy meal: he spoke blessings that made every meal we eat—every meal—holy. He said, "As often as you do this, do it in remembrance of me." The cup he blessed was not encrusted with jewels; it did not have magic powers; it was not of any great value except that it was holy because those who drank from it tasted the kingdom of God.

Christians all over the world have searched for that Holy Grail. They have wandered everywhere and done wonderful and horrible things in pursuit of it. It is on this table today.

—◊—

Some search for the Holy Grail all their lives in lovers, in passions, in churches, in places of refuge, in work or in family. Each time they think that they have found it; or worse yet—much, much worse—think that they can see it in the distance.

It is right in front of them. "The kingdom of God is among you."

Really, truly, it is not that far away. You can hear the kingdom of God twenty minutes before worship as the choir struggles to get the anthem right. You can smell the kingdom of God in the percolating coffee of the fellowship room where parishioners will find unlikely friendships. You can feel it in the cool hand of that quiet woman at the end of your pew.

We are quick to search for the kingdom of God in the particular, in one person, one passion, one place. So we leave today's love for a better love, we discard one passion for a better passion, we search restlessly for one particular church.

All over on this bright morning are Christian churches of every sect and denomination and language, all of them fallen, all short of perfection, yet blessed by a universal meal. Some are drinking from paper cups. Some are drinking from silver chalices. Some are drinking from tiny glasses. All of these containers are holy, and all of these churches are holy, because those who drink are tasting the kingdom of God.

Take a look at the table. The Holy Grail is on it.

Today when you sit down for lunch, take a look at your own table. The Holy Grail will be on it, too. All life is sacramental, all meals are holy, all the world is suffused with the presence and power of Christ. If Christianity needs a Crusade, it needs one that opens our eyes to this accomplished fact.

With all our senses, let us discover today that the kingdom of God is among us—so near that we can taste it.

The Old Rugged Cross

*N*ot all that long ago, the rugged part of our country where I live was cleared and settled by rugged men in hundreds of lumber camps from Clare, Michigan, to the Straits of Mackinac. They were men like Joe Mufraw, who put spikes in his boots in the shape of his initials, and after thirteen shots of whiskey would kick his initials in a ceiling eight feet high.

They worked in winter, long hours from dawn to dusk, in weather forty below. Until 1880, when the crosscut saw was developed, they cut everything with axes. Men even shaved with their axes.

Their bunkhouse had just two very long bunks and two very long blankets. It was a spartan life, but at least they ate prodigiously. A lumberjack's breakfast meant, at the least, fried eggs, pancakes, bacon and potatoes, oatmeal, and coffee. The midday meal might be salt pork, bread and molasses, and tea so thick you could float an axe on it. Each day the cook at Boyne City made twenty-five pies. Your place at the table never changed, nor did you ever talk at the table. You were called to breakfast by a tin horn six feet long; the sound carried three miles, but the bunks were just a few feet away, so you were sure to get out of bed.

At the end of the day, these heroic men delighted in stories of men even more heroic, ten feet tall and taller. They created Paul Bunyan and Babe the Blue Ox, who logged in the period between the Winter of the Blue Snow and the Spring That the Rain Came Up from China. They told about Paul's gigantic cookhouse griddle greased by men who wore pads of butter like ice skates. They told about how the dragging of his pick dug the Grand Canyon; how when he built a hotel, he put the last seven stories on a hinge so they could be swung back to let the moon go by.

Are you all warm and close together? Can you hear the wind howling outside? Then let me tell you a story about a heroic man, a great man, who carried the world upon his shoulders.

You know who I'm speaking of: Simon from Cyrene.

—m—

No, he probably wasn't the man you were thinking of. You were probably thinking of Jesus—a great man, more than a man, who did carry the weight of the world on his shoulders and was the only person ever fit to do it. Others have tried, but only he has been fit.

You were probably thinking of Jesus, but I would like us to think of Simon, who seems, at first glance, unheroic.

Simon came from faraway North Africa to Jerusalem as a tourist for the feast of the Passover. Travel was difficult in those years, and he had probably saved a long time to make his pilgrimage. You can imagine him in his best clothes, visiting the holy shrines, buying souvenirs and temple offerings, paying the money changers at the Temple, unaware that Jesus had disrupted this tourist business a few days before.

He probably had dark skin; he probably looked like a foreigner.

He just happened to be in the street when Jesus and the soldiers came rushing by. He was so absorbed in his own religious experience that he was unaware of the great religious moment in front of him. So there he was—different, completely unaware and unprepared—when Jesus stumbled and the soldiers pulled Simon from the crowd to carry the cross.

> As the soldiers led him away to execution, they seized upon a man called Simon, from Cyrene, on his way in from the country, and put the cross on his back, and made him walk behind Jesus carrying it. (Luke 23:26 NEB)

Simon was the first, but not the last, to carry the cross of Jesus. And he didn't even know what was going on.

—⁓—

Most of us, unheroic people, everyday people, absorbed in our own lives and unaware of the religious moment in front of us, have been asked to carry the cross. It has been the parent who needed care in our home. It has been the child who got into trouble and tested our wits and love. It has been the friend who needed our honesty. You can name the cross. And chances are it hasn't been a shiny polished brass or golden cross. It has been a rugged cross in rugged times.

Jesus carried a rugged cross. So did Simon, and so do we.

I'm sure you can imagine it. It would not have been the whole cross, only the crosspiece for the arms, but still it would have been large, rough and splintery and tremendously heavy. Carrying it was punishment enough. By the time a man was nailed to it, he would have been exhausted, long past resistance.

The soldiers made Jesus carry that cross after he had been whipped, beaten, and crowned with thorns. He was in no condition to carry it. Simon from Cyrene had had no such beatings. He was pulled from the crowd because he was able-bodied, and also for the color of his skin. Imagine the rush in his mind—his confusion, his awareness of mockery, his feeling of injustice to himself, an innocent bystander.

If only he had known what an honor it was to carry that terrible cross.

—⁓—

The Michigan lumber boom ended as this century began. Once the woods were cleared, the jobs moved away. But the legendary feats of the lumberjacks had been impressed on the mind of every boy in Michigan. They heard the stories late at night, when the wind whistled through the cracks in windows, when the boughs creaked beneath the weight of ice and snow. They heard stories of legendary men.

Are you ready for another?

It's about an unlikely hero, an unimposing man named George Bennard. He served in the Salvation Army and then the Methodist Church trying to turn men away from strong drink. He had about as much success as you'd expect, which was very little. Day after day he preached temperance, and night after night men like Joe Mufraw would tie on a few and spike their initials on the ceiling.

A slender man standing all of five feet, three inches, George carried not an axe but a guitar, and made up songs that faded pretty soon after he sang them. He wore longish hair—"poet's hair." Occasionally the crowds heckled him. Undeterred, he sang and preached all over the Midwest, winning many to Christ with his equanimity, warmth, and wit.

In Albion, Michigan, this modest little man began writing a new hymn on his guitar:

> *On a hill far away stood an old rugged cross,*
> *the emblem of suffering and shame . . .*

And on that verse he stayed stuck, for weeks and months. His failure to get any further seemed symbolic, for the revivals weren't going well, and he began to doubt the usefulness of his work.

Usually when he preached revivals he stayed in pastors' homes. One pastor's wife made him feel distinctly unwelcome. After the first night's service and a tense dinner in the parsonage, she told him why. She reproached him for preaching on the cross—divisive and unmodern, she said, and not at all as attractive as the empty tomb of the risen Christ.

But as I say, George was a hero. He refused to miss the religious experience that was right in front of him. Goaded, inspired, he took up that unfinished hymn, and the words now flowed from his pen:

> *To that old, rugged cross I will ever be true,*
> *its shame and reproach gladly bear.*
> *Then he'll call me someday to my home far away,*
> *and his glory forever I'll share.*

It was the one song of his to survive. The first person to admire it was the pastor's wife, a Mrs. L. O. Bostwick, who even paid for the plates to have it printed.

Whoever we are, we may be asked to live heroically. Pressed into service, we take on a burden for a family member or a stranger. We are not strangers to the cross. We know how rough it is and how heavy. We are ready.

Reincarnation

*I*f you were to come back as something, what would you be? Perhaps a cat by a hot stove, or a tree, or a trout? If you were a boa constrictor, you could enjoy a good meal for two or three months. Maybe you could come back as your dog, and your dog could come back as you, and you'd see how you liked *that*.

We Christians know about the incarnation—the miracle of the eternal God becoming a mere man, coming to share our lives first as a humble baby, then as an obscure carpenter among poor people. The idea of *reincarnation* is for us faintly exotic, a curiosity from other faiths. But it holds a fascination for us because it gives bodily shape to an afterlife; it seems so much more satisfying than simply being a spirit; and it leaves us in the known world.

Hinduism and Buddhism teach that all life progresses from the lowest stage to the highest, from plant to animal life, through all the levels of intelligence and right behavior, all the way to human life, building along the way a greatness of soul called *karma,* so that the soul needs finer forms of life in which it can be housed. The only way that you could be a tree or a trout was if you had failed as a human.

The Greeks, who believed in much the same thing, called it the *transmigration of souls.* By one name or another, it has been a persistent idea. It is a way of denying the finality of death—the end of *us*.

—◠◡◠—

173

By contrast, I'd like to tell a great love story born out of loss and grief. It begins with an awareness that death really is the end:

> So the disciples went home again; but Mary Magdalene stood outside the tomb weeping. And as she wept, she peered into the tomb, and saw two angels in white sitting there, one at the head, and one at the feet, where the body of Jesus had lain. They asked her, "Why are you weeping?" She answered, "They have taken my Lord away, and I do not know where they have laid him." With these words she turned around and saw Jesus standing there, but she did not recognize him. Jesus asked her, "Why are you weeping? Who are you looking for?" Thinking it was the gardener, she said, "If it is you, sir, who have removed him, tell me where you have laid him, and I will take him away." Jesus said, "Mary!" She turned and said to him, "Rabboni!" (which is Hebrew for teacher). (John 20:10–18 REB)

He said, *Mary*! And she said, *Rabboni*! You can sense immediately their great love, human love, the passion and beauty of human life.

—⁓—

Easter is all about surprise. The stone was not supposed to have moved, the tomb was not supposed to have been empty, and Jesus was not supposed to be alive. We have never recovered from our surprise.

But there is one surprise we may have overlooked. Perhaps, because we have heard the Easter story since our infancy, we have never imagined it happening any other way. For the people of Jesus' time, and for many people of other faiths today, one thing about this story was a scandal. It was Jesus' reincarnation.

He didn't come back as an angel. He didn't come back with wings. He didn't come back as an eagle, or a dove, or a lion, or a god twenty feet high.

He came back as himself—as an ordinary, obscure man—because that was the point of the incarnation in the first place.

You may have your mouth open to say that Jesus was resurrected, not reincarnated; that he rose from the tomb and stayed on the earth for forty days. Yes, but after Easter even his closest friends did not recognize him. The women at the tomb thought he was a gardener. Two disciples on the Emmaus road walked with him for hours without knowing it. Apostles fishing in a boat did not realize that the man on the shore, giving them familiar directions, was Jesus. It is hard to explain why. Perhaps he did not look like himself. Yet he *was* himself, and whatever his appearance, he appeared to them. He came back for us. He was and is Emmanuel, God with us.

—∞—

Why should Jesus have rejoined us? Why not pass on to a better life with better company and fewer pains? In the words of the Psalm,

> What are human beings that you are mindful of us?
> Yet you have made us little less than gods,
> and crowned us with glory and honor.
> (Psalm 8:4–5, au. trans.)

The incarnation of Jesus' birth was a great surprise—that God became a mere man and shared our lives. And here again, on the other side of death, he reappeared in exactly the same form, to the very people with whom he had already spent his life. Hadn't they already received the full blessing of his presence? You would think so—yet listen:

> She turned around and saw Jesus standing there, but she did not recognize him. Jesus asked her, "Why are you weeping? Who are you looking for?" Thinking it was the gardener, she said, "If it is you, sir, who have removed him, tell me where you have laid him, and I will take him away." Jesus said, "Mary!" She turned and said to him, "Rabboni!"

—∞—

What is heaven like?

For hundreds of years, Christians have spilled great ink and blood over the question of an afterlife. Will we be raised in body or in spirit? Immediately or at the end of time? What kind of immortality awaits us?

Will it be a release from our human natures? Or has Christ shown us, by his incarnation and by the nature of his risen body, what God means for us now and in the next life?

Heaven, as other people have imagined it, does not hold a lot of charms for me. I cringe at the thought of little cherubs strumming harps and ogling each other sexlessly, or walking around on streets of gold for an eternity. But if Deyo and LaVon Beall can find each other again, if Ed and Marie Eichenberger can be together, if mothers and fathers can be reunited with children lost in infancy, if those loves can continue and develop—well, that's another thing altogether. We were made for love, and as pure souls free of wasting bodies, with all the time in the world, maybe we could really know and love each other. Maybe love, which on earth is made precious by our mortality, finds its full worth in immortality.

Maybe that's what heaven is.

—⁓—

Jesus appeared to Mary and called her by name: he said, *Mary!* And she said, *Rabboni!*

In those two words was all the reason for the moment—all the reason for Christ's resurrection, for him, for her, and for us. It was the great love, human love, the passion and the beauty of human life.

—⁓—

Monarch butterflies can be found abundantly this year, as our two-year-old daughter has discovered. Rexene and Hannah brought back from Beaver Island nine caterpillars and a supply of milkweed, put them in a shoebox, and covered the open side with cellophane. Until then I had resisted the charms of butterflies, thinking them too cute and obvious. I can now admit that they are miraculous.

Even the caterpillars are miraculous. Have you ever studied one closely? Perhaps not for days on end. But if it's in a box covered with cellophane on your mantle you will, and you'll be fascinated, I think. When it's ready to make its cocoon, it goes to the roof of the box, then hangs down like the letter J, and writhes and sheds its outer skin to reveal the cocoon, at first as green as a pea pod, which after several days turns gray and jeweled with golden dots.

Watching this metamorphosis is one way of letting a very young child experience death. The caterpillar seeks its own death—or transformation—to become magnificently unlike what it was before. Never again will it be dull in color and creep upon the earth. It will enjoy colorful wings and the freedom of the open air, for another brief lifetime, three or four weeks perhaps. Maybe the afterlife is like this.

And yet, lovely as it is, I would not come back as a butterfly.

If I could come back as one thing, it would be as myself—to be again with Rexene and the friends and family I have loved, to know again the relationships that have defined my self, my very self, to celebrate the miracle of God's love in our lives; and if it is possible, better still to come into a life where I might meet again the loved ones who have died before me—to begin again with my mother, and to meet her mother, and to meet her mother's mother, and all the company of human selves and souls who have ever shaped one another.

That, for me, is a far more glorious life than could ever be known by a bulldog or bullfrog.

The long chain of human memory, human love, passions, passions, passions, is worth death itself, and is the one life beyond this life to which I will dedicate my life now.

On this holiest of days, let us attach ourselves to those we love, and turn to see our old friend standing again before us, calling us by name:

Credits

Several kind and illustrious people have read this book in manuscript. I am indebted to David Buttrick, Thomas Long, and William Willimon.

For the most part I have used the Revised Standard and New Revised Standard versions of the Bible. In some places I have replaced pronouns with names simply for the sake of clarity.

On the other hand, I have elsewhere used male pronouns for God, even though God, of course, is neither male nor female, because English seems clunky without personal pronouns.

Picture Credits

Ed Eichenberger took the photograph of his family's first
home in Dixon.   7

Although the recipe comes from *The Better Homes and
Gardens Cookbook*, the illustrations are my own.   29

This contemporaneous picture of the Peshtigo fire is from
the Wisconsin Historical Society. Reprinted by permission.   45

Many thanks to the Worcester (Massachusetts) Art Museum
for permission to use this version of *The Peaceable Kingdom*,
oil on canvas by Edward Hicks, ca. 1833. Worcester Art
Museum, Worcester, Massachusetts, museum purchase.   66

Mrs. Stuyvesant Fish is the woman on the right. From
Brown Brothers, Sterling, Pa.   87

The photo of Libby and Dan was pasted into a copy of
Libby's autobiography *Child of Sea*, now belonging to
Eleanor Jardine.   106

A snapshot of Jerusalem in snow taken by Sela Yair, an
Israeli photojournalist.   138

From the collection of the London Canal Museum.   143

From the collection of the London Canal Museum.   178

Bibliography

*A*top this bibliography, I acknowledge my chief debt to the authors of scripture—who seem to have authored us.

DIXON, ILLINOIS

Collins, Amy Fine. "Idol Gossips." *Vanity Fair,* April 1997.

Parsons, Louella. *Tell It to Louella.* New York: Putnam, 1961.

Reagan, Ronald with Richard G. Hubler. *Where's the Rest of Me?* New York: Karz, 1965 and 1981.

SWING TIME

Agee, James and Walker Evans. *Let Us Now Praise Famous Men: Three Tenant Families.* Boston: Houghton Mifflin, 1941 and 1960. Excerpt from *Let Us Now Praise Famous Men* by James Agee and Walker Evans. Copyright © 1941 by James Agee and Walker Evans. Copyright © renewed 1969 by Mia Fritsch Agee and Walker Evans. Reprinted by permission of Houghton Mifflin Company. All rights reserved.

Bannon, Lisa. "You'd Think the Injured Party Would Be Ginger Rogers' Family," *Wall Street Journal,* 4 March 1997.

Broydo, Leora."Media Circus." *Salon,* 8 July 1997.

Goodman, Mark. "Keeping the Flame," *People Magazine,* 22 February 1993.

CINNAMON AND SUGAR

May, Rollo. *Love and Will.* New York: W. W. Norton, 1969.

Peck, M. Scott. *The Road Less Traveled.* New York: Simon and Schuster, 1978. Extracted with the permission of Simon & Schuster Adult Publishing Group from *The Road Less Traveled* by M. Scott Peck, M.D. Copyright © 1978 by M. Scott Peck, M.D.

A STICKY SITUATION

Mason, John. "The Molasses Flood of January 15, 1919." *Yankee Magazine*, January 1965.
Park, Edward. "Without Warning, Molasses in January Surged Over Boston." *Smithsonian*, November 1983.

SPLITTING THE ATOM

Brodie, Bernard and Fawn M. *From Crossbow to H-Bomb*. Bloomington: Indiana University Press, 1973.
Stories on the Big Rock decommissioning have appeared in the Petoskey *News-Review* since 1997.

PESHTIGO

Holbrook, Stewart H. *Burning an Empire*. New York: Macmillan, 1943.

THE I.G.A.

For the history of groceries in my town, I am indebted to Eleanor Jardine. *Recently the Harbor I.G.A. was sold and has become Don's Market. You can now find sun-dried tomatoes in aisle two.*

THE PEACEABLE KINGDOM

Ford, Alice. *Edward Hicks: Painter of the Peaceable Kingdom*. Philadelphia: University of Pennsylvania Press, 1998.

LITTLE BLUE BOOKS

Haldeman-Julius, Sue. "An Intimate Look at Haldeman-Julius." *The Little Balkans Review*. Pittsburg, Kans.: winter 1981–82.

MR. JEFFERSON'S BIBLE

Funk, Robert W., Roy W. Hoover, and the Jesus Seminar. *The Five Gospels*. New York: Polebridge Press, a division of Macmillan, 1993.
Hunter, C. Bruce. "Jefferson's Bible: Cutting and Pasting the Good Book." *Bible Review,* February 1997.

Jefferson, Thomas. *The Jefferson Bible: The Life and Morals of Jesus of Nazareth.* Boston: Beacon Press, 2001.

FARMER'S CHEESE

Ammon, Richard. *Growing Up Amish.* New York: Atheneum, 1989.
Hostetler, John A. *Amish Society.* Baltimore: Johns Hopkins University Press, 1980. Excerpt from Hostetler, John A. *Amish Society.* Pp. 306-307, 310-311. © 1980 John A. Hostetler. Reprinted with permission of The Johns Hopkins University Press.

JESUS AND MRS. FISH

Amory, Cleveland. *The Last Resorts: A Portrait of American Society at Play.* New York: Harper and Brothers, 1952.
Auchincloss, Louis (text). *Deborah Turbeville's Newport Remembered.* New York: Harry N. Abrams, 1994.
Balsam, Consuelo Vanderbilt. *The Glitter and the Gold.* New York: Harper and Brothers, 1952.
Lehr, Elizabeth Drexel. *"King Lehr" and the Gilded Age.* Philadelphia: J. B. Lippincott, 1935.
Strange, Michael. *Who Tells Me True.* New York: Charles Scribners' Sons, 1940.

CROSS AT THE LIGHT

Troy, Judy. "Ramone." *New Yorker,* 25 November 1996. Copyright © 1996 by Judy Troy. Reprinted by permisison of Georges Borchardt, Inc., for the author.

A LIGHT IN THE HOUSE

Williams, Elizabeth Whitney. *A Child of the Sea.* Ann Arbor, Mich.: Edwards Bros., 1905.

I'LL BE HOME FOR CHRISTMAS

Lyrics reprinted by permission of Gannon & Kent Music. © 1943 renewed.

GETTING THE HELL OUT

DeKok, David. *Unseen Danger: A Tragedy of People, Government, and the Centralia Mine Fire.* iUniverse.com, 2000.
Glover, Lynne. "Mine Fire Still Rages beneath Tiny Town." Pittsburgh *Tribune-Review,* 3 May 1998.

Thanks to Joseph H. Foster for the anecdote of Walter Jackson.

SNOW IN JERUSALEM

King, Laura. Associated Press Worldstream, 12 January 1998.
Rodgers, Walter. "Rare Snowfall Puts Freeze on Jerusalem's Problems." CNN.com, 12 January 1998.
Rudge, David. "Snow Blankets Capital." Jerusalem *Post,* 12 January 1998.

ONE HUNDRED TONS OF ICE

Bean, Susan S. "Cold Mine." *American Heritage*, July/August 1991.

HERE TODAY

Audubon, J. J. *Ornithological Biography, vol. I.* Edinburgh: 1831–39, 321.
Schorger, A. W. *The Passenger Pigeon: Its Natural History and Extinction.* Madison: University of Wisconsin Press, 1953.
Sharkey, Reginald. *The Blue Meteor.* Petoskey, Mich.: Little Traverse Historical Society, 1997.

THE OLD RUGGED CROSS

Beck, Earl Clifton. *Lore of the Lumber Camps.* Ann Arbor, Mich.: University of Michigan Press, 1948.
Carey, Dan. *Tales of a Michigan Lumberjack.* Mount Pleasant, Mich.: privately printed, 1959.
Holbrook, Stewart H. *Tall Timber.* New York: Macmillan, 1943.
Several towns claim to be the birthplace of George Bennard's famous hymn. The truth seems to be that he wrote it during his travels. I have relied on Molly Shaffer of the Old Rugged Cross Church Museum in Pokagon, Michigan, and Fred Smith of Niles, Michigan. The Rev. Smith was a boy when George Bennard stayed with his family, and was later his clergy colleague.

Notes

1. James Agee and Walker Evans, *Let us Now Praise Famous Men* (Boston: Houghton Mifflin, 1941, 1960), 15.

2. M. Scott Peck, *The Road Less Traveled* (New York; Simon and Schuster, 1978), 119.

3. *New York Times,* 16 January 1919, p. 4.

4. Harry Truman addressed the nation on August 6, 1945.

5. Sue Haldeman-Julius, "An Intimate Look at Haldeman-Julius," in *Little Balkans Review* (Pittsburg, Kans.: winter, 1981–82), 3.

6. Ibid., 4–5.

7. Ibid.,18.

8. Ibid., 19.

9. Letter from Thomas Jefferson to Dr. Benjamin Rush, 21 April 1803.

10. Ibid.

11. John A. Hostetler, *Amish Society* (Baltimore: Johns Hopkins University Press, 1980), 306–7, 310–11.

12. Cleveland Amory, *The Last Resorts: A Portrait of American Society at Play* (New York: Harper and Brothers, 1952), 175.

13. Louis Auchincloss, *Deborah Turbeville's Newport Remembered* (New York: Harry N. Abrams, 1994), 10.

14. Judy Troy, "Ramone," *New Yorker* (25 November 1996): 105.

15. Elizabeth Whitney Williams, *A Child of the Sea* (Ann Arbor, Mi.: Edwards Bros., 1905), 24–25.

16. Ibid., 213.

17. Thomas Carlyle quoted in Huston Smith, *Religions of Man* (San Francisco: Harper Perennial, a division of Harper Collins, 1986).

18. Walter Kent, Kim Gannon, and Buck Ram, "I'll Be Home for Christmas."

19. Susan S. Bean, "Cold Mine," *American Heritage* (July/August 1991): 74.

20. An 1857 committee reporting on a game bill to the Ohio State Legislature, in A. W. Schorger, *The Passenger Pigeon: Its Natural History and Extinction* (Madison: University of Wisconsin Press, 1953), 225.

21. Witmer Stone writing in *Auk,* XXXI (1914), 567, quoted in Schorger, 223–24.